# What Do Grandparents Mean to You?
## (from My Grandchildren)

*Grandparents mean I always have someone on my side,*
*even when I am arguing with my parents.*
Megan, 21

*My grandparents are generous and always go the extra mile for me.*
*They are unspoken authorities and never ground me.*
Cami, 19

*Grandparents are a vacation away from the rest of the world.*
*When they are around, I am not judged; I'm just completely myself.*
McClain, 19

*They are my legacy and anchor.*
Hudson, 17

*Wise friends.*
Builder, 15

*Grandparents encourage you and are always open to you.*
*They are like "backup" parents.*
Kruesi, 13

*They provide a safe place to be, have fun playing with us, and create fun*
*projects that we wouldn't be a part of if they weren't around.*
Beata, 12

*Grandparents mean more people to come to school plays.*
Taylor, 11

*It is so fun when we go to their house . . . it's a lot of happiness.*
Eden, 9

*For loving.*
Ella, 7

*I like it when he [Ross] looks for fish with me.*
Coen, 5

*Love.*
Rainey, 3

*He [Ross] talks to me.*
Gus, 2

*Blessed are the peacemakers, for they shall be called sons of God.*
Blaine, 2
*(Blaine had been reading a book on Bible verses*
*prior to answering this question.)*

HOW TO REALLY LOVE YOUR GRANDCHILD

# How to Really Love Your Grandchild

## ...in an Ever-Changing World

# D. ROSS CAMPBELL, M.D.
### WITH ROB SUGGS

**Regal**

**From Gospel Light**
**Ventura, California, U.S.A.**

Published by Regal
From Gospel Light
Ventura, California, U.S.A.
www.regalbooks.com
Printed in the U.S.A.

Library of Congress Cataloging-in-Publication Data
Campbell, D. Ross, 1936-
How to really love your grandchild . . . in an ever-changing world / Ross Campbell
with Rob Suggs.
p. cm.
ISBN 978-0-8307-4666-8 (hard cover) — ISBN 978-0-8307-4750-4 (international trade paper)
1. Grandparenting. I. Suggs, Rob. II. Title.
HQ759.9.C33 2008
306.874'5—dc22
2008010906


1 2 3 4 5 6 7 8 9 10 / 15 14 13 12 11 10 09 08

Rights for publishing this book outside the U.S.A. or in non-English languages are
administered by Gospel Light Worldwide, an international not-for-profit ministry.
For additional information, please visit www.glww.org, email info@glww.org, or write to
Gospel Light Worldwide, 1957 Eastman Avenue, Ventura, CA 93003, U.S.A.

To my grandchildren

# Contents

# Foreword

The radical social changes in American culture over the past 50 years have left many contemporary grandparents confused about their role. Because of the mobility of Western society, many grandparents live thousands of miles from their grandchildren. Others, because of fractured relationships, are estranged from their adult children and grandchildren. Grandparents who have regular contact with their grandchildren often find that their own ideas of parenting and the ideas of their adult children are different. These differences sometimes lead to conflicts. Given these realities, the question is, "What's a grandparent to do?" In this book, Dr. Ross Campbell answers that question.

Most grandparents genuinely love their grandchildren. They are excited when they are born and follow with great interest their development through the years. They are pained when, for whatever reason, they are unable to see their grandchildren. Grandparents find great pleasure in spending time with them, and when the visit comes to a close, they may be physically exhausted, but it is a happy exhaustion.

However, many grandparents have little understanding about the culture in which their grandchildren are being reared. They operate with paradigms of a former generation that may have little meaning to their grandchildren. Thus, there is often an intellectual and emotional disconnect between grandparents and their grandchildren. Sincerity is not enough. We need information on how to connect with our grandchildren so that the love that is in our hearts may be communicated to their hearts.

Psychiatrist Ross Campbell, who has invested more than 30 years in helping parents and grandparents connect with their children, has done all of us a great service in writing *How to Really Love Your Grandchild*. As a grandfather, I have read it with great interest. The insights and practical advice on these pages are needed by every grandparent who sincerely wishes to leave a positive legacy for their grandchildren. Dr. Campbell shows us how to be successful in that pursuit. In his former writings, he has helped millions of parents effectively rear their children. In this volume, he brings that same wisdom to the task of grandparenting. I am honored to recommend a book that I believe will help thousands of grandparents do what they genuinely desire to do: *really love their grandchildren.*

Gary D. Chapman, Ph.D.
Author of *The Five Love Languages* and
*The Five Languages of Apology*

# 1

New Grandparents for
a New World

Like most adults captured off guard by middle age, Jim and Maggie were youngsters on the inside with a few wrinkles on the outside when they joined the ranks of the world's proud grandparents. They could remember looking upon others who were grandparents as "those old people." They still had a lot of living to do: goals to reach and satisfaction to seek. Now they knew the shocking truth: By golly, becoming a grandparent could happen to anyone!

It seemed as if hardly any time at all had passed since Jack, their son, was no more than a toddler. Somehow that little fellow had grown up, flown from the nest and begun a promising business career. Having also married and started a family, Jack was a genuine, fully certified adult. Jim and Maggie could no longer deny it. Even so, they never truly felt the reality of being grandparents until that first moment when they held little Jared. For the first time, they understood what put the "grand" in grandparenting. Jack had done a brilliant job in providing his parents with such an adorable baby boy. (Maryanne, Jack's pretty wife, had certainly had something to do with this astonishing achievement as well.)

It wasn't long before Jim and Maggie once again discovered the bittersweet truth of how rapidly children grow. Jared began to crawl, then to pull up on the furniture; in no time, he began to stand, to walk, to talk and to wear "big boy underwear" rather than diapers. It would have been nice if the child could have remained a cuddly tot for just a little longer, but his ensuing ages and stages carried their own grandparenting delights. Jim and Maggie loved playing with Jared, reading fairy tales to him and sharing their memories about the long-ago days when Jared's daddy was a little boy.

Being a grandparent, it turned out, was a time for celebration bursting with joy and pride. For years it brought nothing but pleasure, until Jim and Maggie had to serve as temporary *parents* again. For a while, that experience took the "grand" right out of the equation.

Jack and Maryanne had an opportunity to participate in a mission trip to a primitive region of Brazil. The journey required them to be out of the country for four weeks. Taking Jared wasn't an option, so the grandparents were called in to make everything possible. This allowed 10-year-old Jared to sleep in his own bed and attend his fifth-grade classes without disruption. Jim and Maggie were happy to serve. They had no idea they were about to face the phenomenon known as culture shock.

They had enjoyed seeing their grandchild on holidays and special days, most of which were observed on the elders' home turf. Grandmother and Granddaddy enjoyed hosting gatherings for the extended family. Now, however, Jim and Maggie were the "visiting team." They got an up-close and personal look at the daily environment of a 10-year-old at the beginning of a new millennium, and it was unfamiliar territory.

The first enigma involved what was appropriate for a child's television viewing. On this and other matters, Jack and Maryanne had failed to leave detailed instructions—understandably, they'd been preoccupied with international travel preparations.

It suddenly seemed as if every television channel had content that seemed out of bounds for a young viewer. What was particularly troubling was the extent to which Jared seemed perfectly comfortable with these things. The grandparents tried to interest him in channels and programming geared to children, but he wanted to watch the shows that everyone was talking about at school. Jim and Maggie weren't certain what to do. They decided to err on the side of caution, telling Jared there would be certain rules for this particular month; afterward, he could take up the matter with his parents.

Then there was the matter of Internet activity. Jim and Maggie were particularly uncomfortable with this issue, because they knew so little about computers or the Internet. However, they'd heard the horror stories about the world of cyberspace, where censorship didn't exist. They noticed that Jared was already using such features as "chat rooms" and instant messaging. As a matter of fact, this little boy already had his own cell phone!

The grandparents suddenly realized that today's environment was a brand-new world for children—a world driven by rapidly developing technology. Jared liked using his father's laptop computer, so Jim and Maggie made this rule: no computer activity alone. Bring the laptop into the family room where an adult is present.

Then one of Jared's friends invited him over to spend the night. That seemed familiar and innocent enough—at first. When Jim and Maggie asked questions about the friend's family, they discovered that the boy was living with his mother and his mother's boyfriend. This was certainly an issue that had never come up when Jared's father was a little boy. Jim and Maggie were not eager to ask the mother questions, but it looked like they would have to get involved. It sounded as if the adult boyfriend was an occasional resident of the home. Moreover, there seemed to be other unhealthy elements such as heavy drinking and adult parties.

When the grandparents explained to Jared why he couldn't accept the invitation, he grew very upset. He said he wished Grandmother and Granddaddy had never come to stay. These words, of course, were hard for Jim and Maggie to hear. At the same time, they wondered what Jack and Maryanne would do in these situations. Had the world changed so much? What was it like for parents to be confronted by these tough questions on a daily basis?

## GRANDPARENTS: THE NEXT GENERATION

Have you ever felt the culture shock that Jim and Maggie experienced? How would you have handled these issues?

It's true; the world has radically changed. Most grandparents have led fruitful, busy lives without realizing just how revolutionary these changes have been.

Sure, change is constant; every generation is a little different from the one before it. Fashions vary, culture shifts and technology evolves. But today's grandparents have seen the most rapid and unsettling changes of any generation of grandparents before this one.

Think about your own grandparents and their time. They may have seen many historical landmarks: the advent of the automobile, for example. While there were new inventions and new possibilities, however, the basic *culture of the family* remained fairly consistent. From, say, the 1800s through the 1950s, our American life had certain elements at its center: family, small towns, church attendance. Your grandfather was more likely to work in one career, perhaps two, for his entire adulthood. He was probably married once, permanently. And unless he had a military career, he probably lived in one location for the bulk of his life. There were many superficial changes in the way people lived over the years, but the core values remained dominant. Your grandparents lived them out in much the same way their grandparents did.

There was a solid consistency to the generation of our grandparents and their world. Even through the Great Depression that lasted from 1929 through the advent of the Second World War, our predecessors seem "strong and silent" as we look upon them today. Their children, who fought that war, are now called, after Tom Brokaw's book, the "greatest generation." No one claims that they were perfect. But they came home from a destructive war and devoted themselves to construction. They built the most prosperous era in our history, including thriving businesses, families and church denominations. They echoed the values of their parents, centered in the Judeo-Christian foundations of this country's heritage.

But a new age dawned in America with the maturation of the children they raised. During the late 1960s, a theme of rebellion gained momentum. The baby boomers, who are now the ones advancing to grandparent status, began to challenge long-held values. Mass media, dominated by the television set, gradually began to represent new, more liberal, views in nearly every area: religion, politics and sexuality, for example.

## GOOD NEWS, BAD NEWS

Before I say much more, I want to offer you a warning and a promise. The warning is that we're going to discuss some very daunting challenges in this chapter and in this book. What I wish for you to understand—what all of us absolutely *must* understand for the sake of those we love—is that the world around us has changed in some very disturbing ways. If we choose to look the other way simply because we find the subject unpleasant, we severely limit our ability to help our children and our grandchildren. The subject of this book is grandparenting in the time in which we find ourselves. You could certainly read a book on this subject written 30 years ago, and it might provide a more delightful reading experience. But would it give you the timely information you need? We can't address twenty-first-century problems using rusty old tools.

On the other hand, here is my promise: While the challenges of this new and dark culture are disturbing, I find that my doubts are overcome by hope. We are going to find over and over again in these chapters that for every new problem, there is some new and fresh gift that is unique to our times. For example, many of us must be grandparents from a distance. On the other hand, we have the wonderful new opportunity of video messaging by computer. And cellular phones offer long-distance rates that are far lower than they were years ago. Grandparents can see and talk to their grandchildren nearly every day.

That's why I ask for your patience and courage, particularly in this opening chapter, as we talk about the problems we must face. We have to be very honest, very informed and particularly willing to engage those realities. But the truth is that this is still our God's world. He hasn't gone anywhere. Our grandchildren may not spend as many hours at the church as we did at their age; they may not find God precisely in the same ways that we did. But God is at work in fresh new ways. He loves your grandchildren, and your children, just as you do. He wants to bless them, and He wants to bless you. Ultimately this is a book of hope and encouragement, even in a time that can be very frightening and discouraging.

You have already demonstrated that you're a loving and caring grandparent. You've picked up this book, haven't you? Wise decision! You could be reading a magazine or a novel, but you have chosen to equip yourself to be the best resource you can be to the young life or lives that are your pride and joy. That's why I know that we can have an honest discussion about the realities of this world without being discouraged. We know that God is on our side. We are eager to serve Him and serve the ones we love.

All clear on that? Then let's take a closer look at why and how our world has changed—and what that means for your grandchildren.

## GOODBYE, MAYBERRY

When I speak to audiences about the changes we've experienced, I nearly always use the example of *The Andy Griffith Show*. Baby boomers grew up with that television show, and the reruns remain popular more than four decades later. This situation comedy, like many of its kind, celebrated the place of the family, the joy of the community and the power of wise parenting. It showed a community, the small town of Mayberry, where people knew and cared about each other. Such a small-town world, with its slow-paced living and virtuous leaders, now seems like a fantasy. But the fact is that such an America once existed—no, not with perfect people, but at least people who agreed on basic traditional virtues and the centrality of raising children well.

Our country did not step into its future overnight. It has changed gradually since the middle of the twentieth century. I believe that most grandparents don't realize just how drastically these changes have taken place, because they are the elder ambassadors from a different kind of America. You may say, "Actually, I'm a product of those changes. I'm a baby boomer myself." But that's a little deceiving actually. While those who were born between 1946 and about 1964 were raised in the eye of that cultural storm, they were still raised by parents from a simpler and more stable time.

Let's use another example from television. The boomers, known as the first generation raised in front of the television, watched *Andy Griffith*, *Leave It to Beaver*, *My Three Sons*, and a little later, *The Brady Bunch*. Those shows always had a moral center to them, even through the comedy—a spoonful of sugar to help the medicine go down. Now think about what shows were popular 20 to 30 years later. I was shocked by the contrast several years ago when I was cleaning out some old boxes from storage in my home. I came across a videotape that wasn't marked. Curious to find out what was on it, I popped it into the VCR. It was a typical night of TV broadcasting from the mid-1980s, when my kids had been following those shows. These episodes came just about a generation after *Father Knows Best*, yet I was impressed by how they still taught simple lessons about life: being honest, being loyal, treating others fairly.

As late as the 1980s, we took that aspect of our entertainment for granted. Though you may have listened to rock music, worn bell-bottoms and reflected the colorful time that was the 1960s and early 1970s, you were still taking in a lot of traditional values. Your parents drummed those values into you. So did television and other kinds of media.

No longer do the forces of popular culture look out for the character formation of our grandchildren. Role models for girls, for example, are often pop singers along the line of Britney Spears, whose lyrics and presentation are sexually explicit. TV situation comedies are filled with sexual innuendo and immorality played for laughs. The rating system for motion pictures has readjusted itself year by year so that today's PG-13 movie was last year's R-rated film. As I write these words, Hollywood is promoting a new "family" film aimed at children and featuring the eventual death of God. The villains of the piece are clearly drawn caricatures of the Christian ministry, and the author is a militant atheist.

Many children spend hour after hour either on the Internet, where unhealthy influences are everywhere, or playing computer games. Parents and grandparents often have no idea what kinds of influence are involved with their children and grandchildren. In one of the most popular video games, for example, the child plays the part of a car thief. After taking the automobile, he takes off on a virtual reality crime spree, shooting down pedestrians and assaulting anyone in his path.

There is a great deal of ongoing discussion on the extent of influence such games, movies and television shows can have on the formation of a young mind and attitude. Evidence certainly indicates that nothing positive, and very much that is negative, comes from such media. This much is certain: If powerful corporations didn't believe that images on a screen could change human behavior, they would never spend billions of annual dollars on advertising.

## DOES IT REALLY TAKE A VILLAGE?

You're aware of many of these things, of course. It's not breaking news that the world has become a darker and more cynical place. You've seen the evidence on Fox News or CNN. But what you may not have fully considered is just how vastly different is the world surrounding your grandchildren compared to your own world when you were growing up, and even that of your children's world. Have you really taken the time to think about the influences your grandchild faces every day? You may take for granted such obvious truths as the Golden Rule, the Ten Commandments and the simple virtues, and the values that once surrounded any child growing up in our country. But we simply cannot assume that these essential lessons pass through the bloodstream, from one generation to the next.

There's nothing genetic about them. We must teach them these values—and yes, the job of teaching isn't accomplished in a vacuum by parents. During the first years of life, Mom and Dad enjoy having almost a monopoly on the attention of their child. They can determine nearly every detail of what the child sees and hears. But once the school years begin, that child is increasingly exposed to other people and other influences. By the teenage years, the child has a peer group and a little world of his or her own. He or she can make certain decisions about what kind of friends to make at school, which music to listen to and how to spend free time. It becomes harder for parents to guide television and movie choices, though of course Mom and Dad must continue to provide that guidance.

The simple fact is that parents (and grandparents) can do a wonderful job of loving, nurturing and training a child in the way that he or she should go—but the outer world will also have a powerful voice. In the America of 50 years ago—in "Mayberry" America—communities had a powerful positive influence on children. Grandparents, of course, were one important part of that community. When a child visited at her friend's house, for example, the friend's mother could discipline the visiting child. Adults in a community tended to know all the children. But even if they didn't, there was an understanding that they could help each other in the proper training of children.

Think of this scene that might have happened several decades ago, in a department store. A little girl wanders away from her mother. She walks into the toy section and sees a doll in an attractively wrapped package. She begins to unwrap the package and remove the doll. When walking by, you might have stopped and confronted the child, gently asking her to stop what she was doing. You would explain that it's inappropriate to handle things that don't belong to us, and you'd inquire where her mother might be—just a simple moment, but one in which an important lesson was reinforced by a stranger.

Have you thought about how that situation might play out in today's world? For many reasons, the passing stranger would never intervene in this day and age. For one thing, there are so many more legal implications. We're afraid of what someone might say if they see us touching or addressing a child we don't know. And if there is one lesson children are picking up, it's that they are *not* to talk to strangers. There are good reasons for that, since we're so much more aware of predatory behavior. The price we pay, however, is that children miss out on the community experience of learning how to behave socially. Parents, many of them now single, have the additional burden of bearing that responsibility without other adults watching their backs.

An African proverb that has become politicized still carries a certain degree of truth: "It takes a village to raise a child." I'm not talking about delegating the sacred responsibility of a family to government programs; it's simply the idea that in the church, the neighborhood, the playground and the marketplace, parents cannot be in all places at all times. What we can do is help each other out. I'll keep an eye out for your child and his behavior if you'll keep an eye out for mine.

## CHILD-UNFRIENDLY

There was a time when we did a better job helping each other out because the world was far more child-friendly. During the 1950s and early 1960s, our nation was busy raising kids. There were fewer working mothers, of course, so naturally the mother's attention was predominantly on her home. Daycare centers were harder to find; Mom played with her children during the day. She drove the kids to Little League games, Boy Scout and Girl Scout troop meetings, Sunday school classes, the local swimming pool. Such places had communities of parents who took turns helping with each other's children.

It went without saying that newspapers were family newspapers. Television shows in the early evening had to be suitable for family entertainment. We took it for granted that children were at the center of our culture, and therefore we wanted that culture to be clean and wholesome in every way.

Why exactly did that change? For one thing, we've followed the numbers. That huge generation of baby boom children became a huge generation of teenagers, then young adults. As they reached each new age range, popular culture catered to them. It simply made financial sense to do so. In the 1950s, America made bicycles, hula hoops and Davy Crockett coonskin caps. In the 1960s, rock 'n' roll music and youthful fashions made money.

But in the 1970s, that generation did something unprecedented: it prolonged adolescence. The age of marriage began to spike upward so that our children might not marry at 18, but at 28. There were fewer children to worry about, but massive numbers of recreation-driven, affluent young adults. So our popular culture became more sophisticated. Sexuality was addressed more frankly. It became a rock-solid truth that sex and violence made big money, first in the movies and eventually on television.

In our present time period, we find ourselves, in my judgment, in an anti-child culture. Have you watched television with a child lately? I don't mean simply at night, but at any time of day. No longer will the networks or your local station protect children from seeing or hearing inappropriate things. Even mainstream television commercials are sexually suggestive. If you walk with your grandchild in a public place—for example, the local mall—it's now very common to hear adults using profanity with no concern about the young ears nearby. Again, compare these times to bygone years, when children were respected and nurtured almost instinctively.

I hope these paragraphs don't come across as simply another round of moaning about "the good old days." No time period is perfect, of course. The Bible tells us that all of us are sinful and, at the basic level, people do not change. There are good ideas and good opportunities today, and there were bad ones in the mid-twentieth century. But we need to face facts: our culture is largely crumbling. It has lost its moral compass, and most researchers agree that religion and the church are no longer the powerful influences that once guided our society like great beacons.

In particular, it is children who are at risk today. In any time, they are the youngest and most defenseless of all people. Today there are so many dangers around them. It's tougher for their parents, who must struggle in a competitive business environment and a staggeringly expensive time to own a home. There is the factor of divorce, meaning that many children are being shuttled between households or simply raised by one parent. We even see increases in bullying and other threatening behavior among children. Add to these factors the pernicious influence of the mass media, and we realize that the health and wellbeing of our children is in serious jeopardy.

## RELUCTANT GRANDPARENTS

There is one other painful element that I've noticed about today's world. While many wonderful grandparents are stepping forward to make a profound difference, we also must admit that there are a few who don't relish their special opportunity.

Why would a grandparent be reluctant to enjoy the fruit of their autumn years? It could be a number of reasons. Some grandparents are simply tired of parenting. Their mindset is, "We've taken our turn, and we're finished. We want to enjoy our lives now, because we believe we've earned it. Please don't call us unless it's an absolute emergency."

Others have been enticed by this youth-driven culture with its relentless message that life is only for the young. They are terrified of being left behind, of becoming irrelevant. Or they may simply be afraid of old age itself. Consequently, they would rather the world not know they've become grandparents.

Still others are reluctant to fulfill this role because they're uncertain about their relationship with their adult children. Perhaps there is unfinished emotional business there. Maybe forgiveness needs to be granted on one side or the other. There is every reason to make peace for its own sake, of course, but if there were ever a good time for making peace, it would be now. Parents are struggling; they need the help of a loving grandparent.

I trust you're not among any of these categories; otherwise I doubt that you would be reading a book to help you better love your grandchildren. You want to do your best in the difficult and challenging world we've been describing. So where to now? Are there any signs of hope?

Yes there are. Read on.

## SOME THINGS NEVER CHANGE

We've talked about how the world has changed. We've seen that you can't do grandparenting in the same way your grandparents did—so many factors are completely different from when you were a child.

But consider this: Culture changes, but people and their needs do not.

What that means is that your grandchildren still have the same basic emotional needs that children have always had. While the world may be an unfamiliar place, your grandchildren are the same wonderful young creations that God has always placed in our midst. They may listen to strange music sometimes, and there may be earphones plugged into their ears. They may know how to operate a computer better than you do. But children are still absolutely wonderful. They still want desperately to be loved, because God placed that need within them. And they will still respond to grandparents who reach out to them with affection and acceptance.

If you truly love your grandchild—and what grandparent does not?—you can have a terrific relationship with your grandchild. It will be among the most rewarding friendships of your life, coming as it does in the autumn of your life.

I write from personal experience. As we grow older, our children leave us and begin their families. We're so proud of them, and yet our hearts are breaking. Their old bedrooms are silent and empty. We no longer hear their young voices echoing through the house, and we experience a certain craving to be around young people again. Even at church, there's a great deal of age segregation—the youth are herded off to their own classes and activities, and the ministers tend to seek younger adults to lead them. We want to be around that energy and vibrancy, but we fear that young people won't be interested in anything we have to say.

And then along come our wonderful grandchildren, the very image of our own children 20 to 30 years ago. They are curious about Mommy's mommy or Daddy's daddy. They seem to love being around us, and we love to cook for them, give them little gifts and show them how we played with their parents when they were little. Our own children enjoy bringing their children to us. It's a point of pride and a brand-new link between us. Art Linkletter once joked that grandparents and their grandchildren get along so well because they have a "common enemy." But the truth is that grandchildren can be a healing medicine between the two older generations, who now have someone new to love—together.

It is probably the case that your son or daughter lives a hectic life and feels the tension of the rat race that is a reality of our culture. More than ever, you have an opportunity to make a profound difference in the life of your child, and that of your grandchild. You can be a resource for supplemental care and emergency wisdom. You can be a comforting presence, assuring your child that things are going to work out all right. You can provide a loving and understanding ear for your grandchild when she is upset and needs someone other than Mom or Dad to listen.

I have young grandchildren as well as a teenage granddaughter. I love playing with the younger ones and spending time with the older one. She and I have a night out once a month. We go out to eat and talk about her life. I've watched her grow from an infant, and we've kept a close relationship at all times. I enjoy hearing all about her life—her hopes, her dreams, her problems. And when she asks for advice, she listens carefully to everything I have to say. I couldn't say whether these times together mean more to me or to her, because both of us derive absolute joy from the loving friendship we have. And as I grow older, I want to stay in the best possible health—heart, mind and body—so that I can do the same for my other grandchildren. I can't wait to see what they'll be like as they grow up, and how much they'll remind me of their fathers, my two sons.

No matter how challenging these times are, that's a measure of happiness that I could never live without. I know that grandparenting means just as much to you, dear reader. There are so many things you can do and truths you can understand that will help you do a wonderful job with your grandchildren.

Let's move ahead, fellow grandparent. Let's trust God to help us understand all that we need to know in becoming His wise and loving servants for those we love the most in this world.

2

# Helping Mom and Dad

John and Gail were feeling much better about being grandparents. Their son Eddie had married a lovely young woman named Janice, and now Eddie and Janice had a daughter named Jade. The only problem was that they lived far away from John and Gail, who could only see their granddaughter two or three times a year.

They had talked about this with their son and daughter-in-law, who were very understanding. Eddie and Janice made arrangements to come for an extended visit each summer, as well as a good length of time during the Christmas holiday. Whenever possible, John and Gail would travel to see their son and his family. They would have been delighted to see the whole clan every single day, but they were realistic. They knew they had to make the most of the opportunities that were presented to them.

During the middle of one of the summertime visits, a wonderful thing happened. For the first time, Gail sensed that she had bonded with her granddaughter. Of course, she had adored the child since birth, but Jade had seemed aloof around her in those first years. A small child can see someone for a few days at Christmas, then six months later forget who that person is. Gail's heart had sunk during the previous summer visit, when the little girl didn't seem to recognize her Nana. At least by the end of that week Jade hadn't cried when Nana held her. But she still tended to ask for Mommy.

This summer, however, things were different. After about the third day, Jade suddenly decided that both her grandparents hung the moon—particularly Nana. Jade had discovered that it was fun to have a new friend around the house. She would take her grandmother by the hand and lead her to the toys. At meals she insisted that Nana occupy the seat of honor, right beside her. Gail's heart soared; it was the very kind of relationship she had always dreamed about having with a granddaughter.

But the oddest thing happened: as this relationship took flight, another one noticeably wavered.

Janice, Gail's daughter-in-law, began to act strangely—almost as if little Jade's aloofness had left her and entered her mommy instead.

One night, Janice prepared Jade for bed, helping her brush her teeth and put on her pajamas. But when they settled down for a "goodnight story," Jade shouted, "I want Nana to read it!"

Narrowing her eyes slightly, Janice said, "Very well." She handed the storybook to Gail, who had come to kiss Jade goodnight. To Gail, it felt as if the temperature in the room had suddenly dropped about 15 degrees.

Anyone could understand what was going on. Children can be fickle; sometimes they get excited about the "new best friend" and prefer that person to anyone in the world, if only temporarily. Parents know this is a passing fancy, but it's only human nature to feel pushed aside.

Gail read the story to Jade, but on the following day, she tried to be particularly sensitive to Janice's feelings, deferring politely to Mommy on every occasion when Jade wanted to do something together. But Gail's over-polite manner only made things worse; Jade insisted on Nana, particularly since Nana was acting differently toward her.

That evening, Gail discreetly made a trip to the grocery store for a few items just before Jade's bedtime. She didn't want another showdown over who read the goodnight story. When she returned home, she sat down beside her daughter-in-law and attempted to smooth things out between them.

"I'm a little embarrassed," she said. "I'm sure you recognize that it's just a typical passing thing for children. No one replaces Mommy and Daddy, and John and I won't be visiting you for much longer."

"Of course," replied Janice, a bit awkwardly. "I know that, and we love having you here—me as much as your son. It's just that this thing with you and Jade could create problems for us after you leave."

"Oh? How is that?"

"Just little things," said Janice. "The way we do things at the dinner table, the way we do things at bedtime, whatever. I know you're not aware of all these tiny issues, but just as an example—we have a little prayer we've taught Jade, and she says it just before we turn out the light. Just now she said that she didn't want that prayer; she wanted the one that Nana used. I know, it's a silly thing, but . . ."

"Not silly at all," said Gail quickly. "I understand completely. Without meaning to do anything of the kind, I can upset the routines and the habits you're trying to teach your daughter."

"I appreciate how understanding you are," Janice said, smiling. "You are a wonderful mother-in-law and a wonderful grandmother." She looked as if an uncomfortable burden had slipped from her shoulders, and the two shared a hug.

"Hey, just doin' my job!" said Gail in a comic voice. And they both had a good laugh.

The next day, Gail added some new strategies to her portfolio. At the dinner table, if Jade said, "I want Nana to sit right here," Gail would make it a point to ask Jade how her mommy liked to arrange the seating. Again she read the bedtime story, but afterward she said, "Let's use the prayer your mommy and daddy have taught you."

She watched carefully and was surprised by how much information she gleaned about the little family's traditions. After that, with every trip, she knew that she was fitting in a little bit better and causing a minimum number of conflicts within the household political system.

## WHEN IN ROME

It's a classic grandparenting issue.

"Would you like a piece of candy?"

The little boy looks sheepishly from Granny to his parents. "Mom and Dad don't allow me to eat candy," he says.

"You're at your granny's house now," says the grandmother, "and *she* says that in her house, all children are permitted to eat candy!"

Mom and Dad grit their teeth as the child learns about this fascinating new galaxy where parents are not the ultimate authority.

As a child begins life, the parents are godlike. Parents determine truth, behavior and all significant rules. Then the child visits a friend's home and discovers, perhaps, that some television shows and video games are permissible after all. He or she goes over the river and through the woods to grandmother's house and learns something even more interesting: grandparents have a kind of power over Mom and Dad; he or she might be able to eat the candy or behave in certain ways *right before a parent's eyes*. A grandparent, who is a loving and a lovable figure, seems to represent a force that trumps the usually unquestioned authority of parents.

It's a kind of generational politics, isn't it? No wonder our grandchildren are puzzled by it; the arrangement confuses us at times too. When you were growing up, you honored your father and your mother, just as the Bible taught. You continued to honor them after you left home, though the relationship may have shifted just a bit. You began to relate to your parents as fellow adults, and in that sense, intellectual equals—though they were still the parents who brought you into the world, loved you and taught you about life. You still understood the importance of deferring to them in the little questions that might arise. For example, when you visited their household, you observed their time-honored traditions and preferences.

Then, when you brought your children to their home, there would be three generations present, and sometimes two sets of rules. The child deferred to his parents, who deferred to their elders. But what if these two sets of rules came into conflict? Candy, or no candy? Do we say a blessing before meals? How late do the kids get to stay up? Most of these are not particularly significant in or of themselves, but they become issues of authority.

There are several questions that need to be acknowledged when the rules of parents and grandparents seem to conflict. One is the basic law of love and respect. No matter what happens, it should always be clear that everyone respects both parents and grandparents; that is, the grandchild respects both levels above him, and his parents continue to respect their own parents. No one need ever undermine anyone else. We don't want to send mixed signals to our children or grandchildren about the honor that is owed to parents and elders. As they obey their moms and dads, they enjoy seeing how their parents do the same thing, one generation upward.

## What Your Grandchild Needs

As a matter of fact, this will be a recurring theme as we talk about grandchildren and their needs: Kids must experience an atmosphere of unquestioned love and as much harmony as possible. There is always going to be a certain amount of tension, because no family is perfect. But the more stress and anxiety linger in the air, the more upsetting it will be to your grandchild. If for some reason you are upset with your child or his or her spouse, you should remember that children have powerful natural antennae when it comes to emotions in the atmosphere. The extended family needs to provide an environment of extended security and love. When a child steps into this household and finds conflict between the two generations above him, it will be very upsetting.

But that can place you, the grandparent, in a dilemma. The problem may not be with you, after all. Your child, the mother or father of your grandchild, may come onto the scene filled with stress. Your adult child may be the one who fails to provide the respect for you, and possibly sets a poor example for the child. What can you do in such a situation?

There may be limits to what you can accomplish at a time like this. You can only truly control your own behavior and reactions. It's effective to remind yourself of your adult child's perspective. If you're tempted to make an angry remark to your adult child or in-law, think about how this comes across to your grandchild. Remember what it's like to be young, to depend on elders for love and security and to hear them squabble with each other.

If you do that, you will find it easier to bite your tongue and be what the Bible calls "longsuffering"—patient and forgiving, and compassionate toward someone who has perhaps been worn down by a hard day. When your grandchild sees you refusing to react temperamentally, and instead you put a comforting arm around the upset one, this will teach a powerful and positive lesson. It will reinforce the impression that this, your home, is a place where people can come to be accepted and loved.

Then, of course, when you have the opportunity to speak outside the hearing of your grandchild, you might be able to say something like this: "I realized you were upset a while ago. I didn't want to do or say anything that might possibly be troubling to you or (grandchild's name). We certainly want to keep things as pleasant and loving when the younger ones are around. That's why I thought it would be best to discuss these things at a different time."

What does your grandchild need the most? A safe and secure place where he will feel loved. When he's away from his own home, he needs to know that his environment will be peaceful. Friction between adults is always upsetting to a child, whether it's between parents or between parents and grandparents. If we could only realize how this feels from a child's perspective—perhaps how we ourselves once felt—I know that we would be far more patient and compassionate with each other as adults.

## Who's in Charge Here?

We agree, then, that children need to see their parents model respect and obedience for elders so that they will respect their own parents. Then, only a few paragraphs later, we suggested that grandparents should be patient and not retaliate when their children are the ones who are "misbehaving." It almost seems contradictory, doesn't it? How does all this fit together?

Certainly children defer to their parents, and parents to their parents. That's how it should work. But as we all know, our families aren't perfect. That middle generation is the one feeling the crunch right now. There will be times when your children are stressed out and burdened by career, by family pressure or by any number of things.

If your adult child walks into your house in a foul temper, for example, or is upset with something you've done as a grandparent, you *could* assert your authority. You could say, "I am your mother (or father)" and insist upon the proper respect. As you can imagine, this would likely make the situation worse. That's why it's best to pick your battles wisely. In front of the grandchild, promote harmony. You're modeling a wonderful disposition for both younger generations when you do that. Then, as we've seen, you can speak to your child more seriously at a later time, when younger ears are not in the vicinity.

There is another point to be made about this chain of authority issue. Who is actually "the boss" in a given situation? Does it depend upon the household, as some believe? In that case, grandparents make the rules at their home; adult children make the rules at their home. Or are the grandparents always in the right because of seniority?

The answer is that, in most, if not all cases, we have to respect our children as parents. For a number of reasons, we wouldn't want to undermine their authority in front of their children. For example, consider the case of the candy. Many doting grandmothers say, "I know your parents don't want you eating sugary foods. But we're in my house now." Or, "When you're staying with your grandparents, you don't have to go to bed so early." Worst of all: "We don't need to tell Mommy and Daddy about this." (Wink) "Let's let it be Gramma's little secret."

I hope I'm not stepping on any toes here. It seems to be a venerable grandparenting tradition to slightly spoil our grandkids. We enjoy showering love on the younger ones. We want them to remember our home as the most wonderful place in the world for a visit so that they're nearly shouting with joy as they bound through our door. We may be trying to pamper them to create that level of excitement about Grandma and Grandpa. We may even have some preconceived negative ideas about how our children are doing as parents, so we're trying to quietly take corrective action on our own.

There are at least a couple of good reasons that you should never go against the wishes of your adult child in his or her parenting role. Number one, of course, is that you're subtly undermining parental authority—even on little things. You won't be there to hear it, but you can be certain that later on, junior is going to say, "Grandma lets us have candy!" There may also be distinct accusations that go like this: "Grandma loves us more than you. She does nice things for us." A parent can spend hours explaining why the rules are what they are; the second that another adult changes the rules, it creates doubt and confusion for the child.

The second issue to consider is that you're harming your relationship with your adult child when you disregard his or her rules. Imagine a situation in which parents know that whenever they take their child to your home, their parenting patterns will be disrupted, even if only in small ways. They might be less likely to visit you.

You might insist that your children don't mind your spoiling the grandchildren, and this may be so. Even so, I believe that children benefit from consistency and clear signals rather than shifting systems and permissiveness; and it's never a good thing when one side can be played against the other.

## Who Loves You Most?

We've already touched upon an issue that often arises between parents and grandparents: competition for a child's affection. There could be many reasons that adults compete for being first in the heart of a child. All of us love being adored by a little one. Sometimes there are adults who, for one reason or another, aren't receiving all the love they deserve from other quarters. There could be a grandparent who has been widowed, and craves the abundant love a child can give. Without realizing it, he or she could try to receive extra attention from the grandchild. Or it may be that there is some unresolved conflict between parent and grandparent—unfinished business from their earlier relationship—that finds expression by making the child the object of competition. Any of these scenarios would be unhealthy situations. Yet they do happen.

Let's revisit the situation of Jade, her mother, Janice, and her grandmother, Gail. Jade abruptly decided that her grandmother was her very best friend, and she centered all her attention on her. Naturally, Gail was delighted; who doesn't enjoy being adored by a child? When Janice demonstrated her unhappiness with this development, she and Gail had a talk. Janice explained it as a function of possibly disrupting the parental rules—the very situation we discussed above. Gail responded cooperatively. She didn't want to do anything to break the patterns of behavior that Eddie and Janice were enforcing in the home.

But it's entirely possible that, in Janice's mind, there was more to it than that. Sheer human nature would account for her irritation in seeing her beloved child seemingly forget that her mommy existed. After all, Janice gave most of the hours in her day to care for Jade. She fixed all her meals, cleaned her room and sacrificed many other things for the child. She would understand that this was a passing thing, typical of children; but Janice still had normal human emotions.

Add to that the factor of her relationship with her mother-in-law. You may have noticed from previous accounts that Gail and Janice met very briefly before Eddie married Janice; then the young couple lived a great distance away. Perhaps the two women weren't completely comfortable around each other. The point is that there are a lot of reasons that parents and grandparents, without quite realizing it, may find themselves competing for the number-one spot in a child's heart.

Of course it's another reason to be careful about pampering our grandchildren. As much as we enjoy their love, we certainly don't want our adult children to feel that we're trying to somehow replace them. And while we're at it, let's remember that no quantity of cookies, stay-up-late hours or anything else will really make a child love you more. Did you fall in love with your spouse because of the gifts you received during courting? Of course not. People love us for who we are. Grandchildren naturally adore their grandparents, as long as the grandparents are warm, affectionate and attentive to them. As soon as they sense that a grandparent can give them toys, sweets and other things, of course, they will begin to push those buttons. It's always healthier to build a relationship based upon the intangibles of love.

The competition problem can rise particularly in cases when the parent(s) and child have moved in with a grandparent, or vice versa. The grandparent begins to do a certain amount of the parenting, and the parent may feel that he or she is "losing" the child. We'll spend a chapter on what happens when grandparents become parents. For now, let's agree that grandparents must be very careful, even in such a living situation, to defer to Mom and Dad. Always make it plain that you are not a third parent or a replacement parent, but an aide to the real ones. You are a resource person. Make that assurance verbally, and show it through your actions. Your adult child will be deeply grateful.

In more traditional situations, when children come to your home for a visit, it's normal for grandchildren to flock to you and even favor you during those special occasions. Just watch to make sure this pleases Mommy and Daddy. In most cases, it will. If your adult children do feel that you're somehow usurping their place, talk it over. Engage the issue directly, and be sure that you're not using the weapon of pampering, or anything else, to gain an advantage.

## TALK ABOUT EVERYTHING

I've mentioned the wisdom of talking to your children when their children aren't around. It sounds obvious, but think about it: It's easy to neglect this simple need. In the hustle and bustle of life, a young family will flood into Grandma and Grandpa's home for a visit, then leave en masse when it's time to go home. You may have missed the opportunity to sit down and talk seriously and privately as grandparent to parent because the children tend to be the center of attention during those visits.

That's why many grandparents come to feel that they know more about their grandchildren than their own children after a period of time passes. We all place the little ones first; but the adult-to-adult relationship needs nurturing too.

I recommend that extended families spend time with each other in various combinations: just grandparents with parents, just grandparents with grandchildren, and then, of course, everyone together. Take your adult children out to dinner regularly, and make it a point to converse casually about how life is going with your grandchildren. Find out how they feel about some of these issues that will come up during visits so that you'll be on the same page. Your children are likely to have different parenting philosophies than yours, because every generation makes its own adjustments and contributions to the ancient art of parenting. Your influence as their mother or father will be present; so will the contributions of your child's spouse; so will the newer trends among parents. Together, these factors add up to a mix that will differ from your way of doing things.

For example, you may have heard about "helicopter parents." This is the tendency for today's parents to "hover" over their children, seemingly monitoring and guiding a child's every move during times that are anxious. When we were younger, there was less reason for worry, and less hovering. The community was more trustworthy, and we received better support from others to raise our larger families. As you listen to your adult child talk about parenting, you'll pick up on the important details. Ask questions: Can you serve snacks? Can the children play outside? How late can they stay up at night? What forms of discipline are preferred?

While you're at it, talk about non-parenting things as well. In the next chapter, we're going to talk about the "love tank," which is the natural reserve of love from others that we have available at a given time. Parents need their love tank filled too. They give and give, sometimes receiving little back from their children or (busy as they are) from each other. An arm around the shoulder and an encouraging word from Mom or Dad goes over particularly well to a struggling parent. You have the opportunity to be a rock of support, a shelter in any storm, for your children. Don't make the mistake of focusing so much on your beloved grandchildren that you forget your own beloved offspring. That's another reason why you need to be intentional about spending time with—and giving love to—your children. That's probably the best gift you can offer as a grandparent.

## How to Give Advice

Gail and her daughter-in-law talk once a week on the phone when they're not together; it helps them stay close even though they live miles apart. She thinks often about how far they've come in their relationship.

Gail made an extended visit to provide support during the first days of Jade's life. Parenting was so new and overwhelming to Janice that the younger woman was always asking questions. For example, "When should I let the baby cry?" "If the baby doesn't seem to be eating quite enough, how soon should I call the doctor?" Those first days as a parent are humbling ones, and new moms and dads tend to eagerly solicit advice from any quarter. But as Jade grew, of course, Janice became more confident in her own judgments. When Jade was slow in potty training, Gail asked a few tentative questions about how Eddie and Janice were guiding the process along. She noticed that Janice wasn't eager to talk about that particular situation. Janice had a strategy, and she was going to stick to it; plus, it was a sensitive issue for Eddie and Janice that had already caused arguments between them. Therefore, Gail made it a point not to raise the subject again.

What has Gail learned? She knows not to be a constant, voluntary dispenser of parenting advice. That's not what Eddie and Janice need most from her. Oh, she has her opinions, all right—everything from potty training to discipline to whether or not to have Jade take piano lessons. Gail knows exactly how she would do things, and most of those ideas have emerged from the hard-won wisdom she gained as a parent. Like most of us, she is well aware of what she did right and what she might have done better in raising her two boys. There's no denying that she is a fount of wisdom on parenting. And sometimes she is aching to simply say, "Let me tell you what I think."

Most of the time, however, she errs on the side of silence. What the young parents need is support and encouragement rather than unsolicited instructions. If a question comes up, Eddie and Janice won't hesitate to ask it of Gail, because they know that she loves them and has many wise observations. They just want to be the ones to initiate the conversation.

For that purpose, those weekly phone chats work like a charm. Gail almost never brings up parenting issues. She simply asks how everyone is doing, including the parents. She shows interest in the whole gamut of family life. From time to time, Janice will tell her about some problem they're having with Jade, and she'll say, "Gail, what would you do?"

It is at those moments that the mother-in-law feels perfect freedom to speak her mind. She's been given the ball, and she runs with it. Even so, she does it in a loving way. She avoids saying things like, "Well, now that you mention it, I have noticed that you're going about this all wrong. I didn't want to say anything and hurt your feelings, but here is how you should have done it." If she spoke like that, it's unlikely she'd ever be asked for advice in the future.

No, even now—even when her daughter-in-law expressly requests her wisdom—Gail understands what Janice needs even more than the practical stuff. She needs an older friend, someone who has fought all the battles, to give her a word of love and encouragement; someone to reassure her that whatever problems young parents may have, they're not particularly unique. Nothing is new under the sun, including the raising of children.

Young parents need unconditional love, just like everyone else. They need a solid foundation of senior advisors who can help them physically, mentally, emotionally and spiritually. And there is no one in the world who can fill that need better than a loving grandparent.

## THE OTHER GRANDPARENTS

Finally, let's take a moment to consider that other entity we often forget: the other set of grandparents.

Most younger children have two sets of grandparents, and I've found that there can be a certain amount of conflict between one side and the other. The child's parents may be married, but that doesn't mean that Mommy's parents are close to Daddy's. The classic time for this kind of tension, of course, is the holidays. Traditions on both sides are almost certain to conflict. The child's parents find themselves involved in sensitive negotiations: "We'll go to your folks' place for Thanksgiving this year, my folks' for Christmas." Somehow these compromises fail to satisfy either side more often than not.

How can you help? Be understanding of the other set of grandparents and their desires. It would certainly be a good idea to meet them and cultivate a friendship if possible. Talk to them about their traditions and ideas for spending time with their grandchildren; share your own. Do everything you can to encourage your adult children to share your grandchildren with both sets of grandparents. Remember that any family tension to which you contribute, in any way, is very painful to the grandchild. Be patient, considerate and unselfish.

# 3

# Grandparenting from a Distance

J ack and Barbara wondered how it was possible to be bursting with pride and to be broken-hearted at the same time. They stood near the international gate at the airport, beyond which they weren't permitted to pass.

They were proud that Jane and Vince, their daughter and son-in-law, were on their way to Brazil to begin their new life as missionaries. Yet they were heart-broken at the thought of the distance that would separate them—especially just as Little Jack was reaching such an interesting age.

Vince and Jane planned on home schooling Little Jack at their new home. He was seven years old, and he loved his grandparents; the feeling was more than mutual. When Jack and Barbara looked at him, they saw a young male image of their daughter. It was already clear that he resembled his mommy in his wide brown eyes as well as his friendly, inquisitive nature. Now they would see their grandchild and his parents only during missionary furlough periods—and those would be anything but regular.

Yet they were fiercely proud of their daughter, of the wonderful man who was her husband and of the life of service they had chosen. Jack and Barbara's church was helping to provide support for the missionary couple, and that meant that Jack and Barbara's friends were interested in news about the little family. When Vince and Jane had come to the church and led a special missions weekend, Jack and Barbara had beamed with pride.

Somehow they hadn't really considered what it would be like when they had to say good-bye for many months. Barbara, the loving mother and grandmother, wept quietly as she held her husband's hand and walked to the car. On the way home, they were too sad to speak. Over dinner, however, Jack broke the silence. "So what are we going to do?" he asked. "How am I going to be a dad and a granddad from the other side of the globe? What about you, honey?"

"I've thought a lot about it," said Barbara. "And I've decided there aren't any simple answers. If we had a private jet and an unlimited supply of fuel, wouldn't life be grand?"

"Probably not," smiled Jack. "You know how it goes when we travel. I would take a wrong turn at Central America, refuse to stop and ask for directions, and you would nag at me all the way."

Barbara had to laugh at that. And she had to admit that it felt good to laugh. But where was Jack going? After his words, he'd risen from his chair and walked down the hall. She could hear him moving things around in the junk room.

Soon he came back with a big box.

"What in the world have you got?" she asked.

"Something to make the world smaller, I hope," her husband replied.

What was in that package? It was no less than the beginning of a wonderful adventure in grandparenting. Let's follow their progress and find out the amazing secrets in long-distance grandparenting.

## Secret Number One: The Power of Email

Jack cut the wrapping tape from the big box. Inside was a brand-new laptop computer.

"Ugh," said Barbara. She was clearly underwhelmed.

"I know that computers leave you cold," said Jack, "so I waited until now, when I knew you would listen to any idea that would bring you closer to Vince, Jane and Little Jack."

"I'm listening," said Barbara without enthusiasm.

"I have created a separate email account for both of us," said Jack. "I've given those to Jane. Of course, they already have email—everybody in their generation does, and nearly everyone in ours, except for you." He smiled as Barbara rolled her eyes. "Tomorrow morning, at breakfast, I'll have two things waiting at your place at the table: a cup of coffee and a full account of our little family's flight and arrival at their new home."

For the first time, Barbara showed real interest. "They can do that? So quickly?"

"That's the beauty of email," said Jack. "We'll have their words a couple of shakes after they write them. And vice versa." He looked closely at his wife, who now seemed to be staring into space. "Anything wrong?" he asked.

"I have to bone up on my typing skills," she said. "I haven't typed a letter since the 1960s!"

Email is a wonderful innovation. If you don't think so, ask anyone who is far away from home. Our soldiers in a distant part of the world can be as close to their loved ones as a typed sentence. Missionaries and business travelers can have access to nearly anyone at any time. The big advantage of email, of course, is that it is so inexpensive and so immediate. Nearly everyone enjoys getting a good, newsy email message from a family member.

Email accounts are free from yahoo.com, hotmail.com, and any Internet service provider that you choose. There was a time when computers and the Internet were the domain only of the young and the techno-savvy. But today there's a good chance that nearly any grandparent reading these words already has an email address and a few favorite Web pages.

With email, you can send a short message every day, if you like. There's an opportunity to share ordinary days with your grandchildren rather than just holidays and special occasions. You can talk about what your grandchild is learning in school, and what kind of friends he has.

And while we're at it, let's say a word or two about that other mode of quick communication, the telephone. If your grandchild lives within the continental United States, you have the opportunity to speak frequently and at length, for a very reasonable monthly fee. This wasn't possible only a few years ago. But the cellular phone revolution has made it cheap and easy to talk over the phone. As a matter of fact, with the right plan, you can even call other countries in an affordable fashion.

If you have a good calling plan, use it to keep in touch with your long-distance family. Once a week is a nice interval for regular calls, but you can make it more, or less, frequent based on your situation. Sometimes we make "whole family" calls, particularly on holidays, when the phone is passed around and a few words are exchanged with each of five or six or seven family members. But I recommend being a bit more strategic. Call one specific party: say, your grandchild. Make sure he knows that you're not simply saying hello as part of a more important call to his parents—he is the reason you're on the phone. This will tell your grandchild how important he or she is to you.

Talk about ordinary things he is interested in. As much as possible, share his world. Your objective is to build such a closeness that he'll always feel comfortable coming to you in a time of need. I have this kind of relationship with my granddaughter. We've remained close ever since she was very small; as a result, she comes to me when she has a problem and needs a grandparent's ear.

Email and phone calls are wonderful gifts—lifesavers in a culture that has separated extended families by greater distances than ever. Can they take the place of physical togetherness? No. But they can make quite a difference.

Let me add another tip that has made a dramatic difference for me. My granddaughter is in college, and what a busy time that is! I've made great use of text messaging to keep in touch with her. She could be in class or busy studying if I made a call from my cell phone. But a text message can quickly be read even in church or during a university lecture. I use these text messages to arrange a time convenient for both of us to talk.

No matter how many activities our collegiate grandchildren have, they always enjoy a conversation with their loved ones. Text messaging is another example of using technology rather than scorning it. If we want to be part of our grandchildren's world, we need to embrace the technology that is so much a part of it.

## SECRET NUMBER TWO: THE POWER OF THE PACKAGE

Jack and Barbara enjoyed the ease and immediacy of email. But one day, Barbara brought her husband a stack of yellow envelopes bound by an ancient rubber band.

"What in the world are these?" Jack asked.

"Letters from my father," Barbara said softly, "written from various parts of Western Europe in 1944 and 1945."

Jack took in a deep breath. "Wow, letters from the front—at the end of World War II. I remember that he fought there, but I didn't know you still had his letters."

"I was a very small girl," said Barbara. "The letters didn't mean much to me at the time. But my parents knew that someday they would. My parents saved each letter for me, complete with the little flower petals and Belgian trinkets and photographs that Dad enclosed."

Jack and Barbara spent several hours reading those letters. Jack hadn't known her father well, but after reading 35 letters, he felt as if he had.

"Do you think Little Jack will feel this way about our email?" Barbara asked.

"Their hard drive crashed last month," Jack said. "I bet they no longer even have copies." The couple looked at each other forlornly.

Barbara said, "Email is so wonderful that the 'E' should be for easy. But there's no rule that we can't do it the old school way, is there?"

The next day, Jack and Barbara had the time of their life as they assembled a big care package. They often sent their daughter little things she couldn't find in Brazil, but it had never occurred to them to make a package just for their grandchild. How special and different it would seem compared to mere electronic words on a computer screen. They enclosed three packages of cocoa, a coloring book, a new book of Bible stories, some fresh fruit carefully packaged and, of course, two handwritten letters—one from each grandparent.

They discussed their letters before writing them. Some of it was the usual simple conversation they might have put in email. But for this more personal, more traditional and longer-lasting medium, they were inspired to do a bit more. Each would write about a day in their lives when they were the age that Little Jack was now. They decided to do that perhaps once a year so that Little Jack would have some of their memories and experiences that paralleled his own age.

Care packages are a wonderful treat for any grandchild. They need not be expensive or fabulously creative—simply heartfelt. Care packages offer a unique element of surprise and delight. They contain tangible items that are personal and memorable. And handwritten letters, of course, are unsurpassed as heirlooms.

My friend Rob loves to tell the story of his grandfather Daddy Bob, for whom he was named. One summer day, Daddy Bob wrote Rob a nice letter with something unexpected: Daddy Bob wasn't an artist, but he knew that Rob liked to draw. He included some hand-traced comic strips from the newspaper, just to show his grandson the technique of tracing as a way to improve drawing skill. It made a deep impression on Rob, one he has never forgotten, and probably had a great deal to do with Rob becoming a professional cartoonist years later. He speaks of how much it meant simply to know that his grandfather thought enough about him to trace cartoons.

The personal touch makes a lasting memory. Even if you use email, I recommend that you write occasional letters with pen and ink—letters that may be saved long after you're gone—and every now and then surprise packages that convey a touch of fun and pleasure.

## SECRET NUMBER THREE: THE POWER OF HUMAN VOICE

Jack and Barbara got a wonderful response after sending their little package. "Little Jack couldn't stop talking about it," Jane told them in an email. "He won't even drink the cocoa because it's too special—he wants to keep his 'grandparent package' all together. We absolutely insisted on eating the fruit, however!"

The pleased grandparents decided they would strike again, but only at unexpected times. They wanted their idea to remain special, and they wanted each mailing to contain something new and different, along with the "memory letters" that would become a staple.

Soon Jack had just the thing. "Did you know that a microphone plugs right into this laptop computer?" he asked.

"Nothing about these computers would amaze me," Barbara replied. "I guess I'll never get used to them."

" . . . about these computers would amaze me," repeated a voice that sounded, well, something like Barbara's. "You recorded me!" she accused, hands on hips. "I don't really sound like that, do I?"

"Most people don't like their recorded voice," said her husband. "But our Little Jack will love ours. Now, why not say a few words for the boy and his parents?"

Barbara would never have thought of such a thing—recording their voices to a 40-minute greeting, then actually making their own compact disk of it! Jack's computer had a disk burner, and he had learned how to save and burn a recording onto a disk. Barbara had to admit, this modern technology might be bewildering, but it had its good points too.

This idea was an intriguing one because it had the personality of the human voice, like a phone call, but the permanence of a letter. Their first attempt was a little bit awkward; Jack and Barbara looked at each other and wondered what they should say. So they turned off the recorder, put their heads together and decided it would be really nice to talk about what Jane, Vince and Little Jack meant to them.

After that decision, the words came very easily. The only problem was that Barbara shed a sentimental tear or two as she spoke from the heart. But that felt pretty good too. They talked about the first time Jane brought home her boyfriend, Vince, for her parents to meet. They described the evening, several years later, when Jane revealed that a baby was on the way. And they shared their favorite stories of playing with Little Jack when he was an infant. Finally, they talked about their dreams for the future. They envisioned Little Jack becoming Big Jack with big dreams, big potential and a big impact on the world through his faith and his wonderful talents.

You can imagine what it meant to the young missionary family to receive this CD filled with recorded encouragement and love. They played it every few months, particularly during times when they were discouraged, and home felt far away. They made extra copies of the CD and had one placed in safekeeping where they would have it forever, long after Jack and Barbara had left this world.

Could you make such a recording? I don't see why not. Not only would you be giving an absolutely singular and unique gift to your loved ones—another legacy for your grandchild—but it would do your heart good to sit down and speak meaningful words of love into the microphone. Many laptop computers have built-in microphones so that there isn't even anything to plug in. This book was prepared with such a computer microphone.

## Secret Number Four: The Power of Home Video

Well, you know how one thing leads to another, right? By this time, Jack and Barbara had caught the technology bug. So much excitement was generated by their unexpected surprise packages that they wanted to come up with something new and different with every mailing.

Barbara did the research this time. She and Jack had not owned a movie camera since the old Kodak Super 8, which was stuffed away in a closet somewhere. But it turned out that no expensive video cam was necessary after all. Once again, computers came to the rescue—was there nothing they couldn't do?! Many computers have simple motion cameras built in; if yours doesn't have one, any store that has camera components will sell a simple and inexpensive camera attachment for your computer. The hard disk saves the video as a file, and it can be attached to email or, again, burned to a video disk. It's all very simple—trust me on this!

Jack and Barbara enjoyed making a home video, much like the audio recording they'd made earlier. This time, however, they could be much more creative. They took the laptop and the video cam to church and had various people film short greetings. Later, after borrowing a proper video camera, they were able to drive through town and film special places that Little Jack, and his mommy and daddy, loved. Then they had a wonderful time putting all of this together on the computer and burning it to a special disk. Computers today come with video editing software that makes all of it a snap.

Many families use computer cams to see each other's faces as they speak over the Internet. When my son took his family and moved several states away, I learned how to enjoy this option. At first the video was fairly poor in quality; but things are getting better all the time, especially with the advent of broadband Internet.

Isn't it wonderful that your grandchild could live across the world, and you could still have a face-to-face sit-down conversation?

# THE POWER OF TOGETHERNESS

If you're facing the prospect of grandparenting from a long distance, I hope I've sufficiently made the point that modern technology, wrapped in love and packaged with creativity, can help to make the miles seem fewer. As a matter of fact, that same technology can help you document your memories and create keepsakes that your grand-child will treasure forever.

But no technology, no matter how advanced, will ever substitute for being in the same place at the same time. In times past, grandparents and extended family were often very close at hand. It's not always the case today. Therefore, we must make the most of the opportunities we do have. Allow me to make some recommendations to enhance those precious occasions when you can be with your beloved grandchildren.

## Family Reunions

In recent years, as families have scattered across the map, reunions have become more popular than ever. Many resorts, hotels, parks and bed-and-breakfasts cater to family reunions. You can find a good weekend or holiday time to plan a reunion if you plan well in advance (at least 12 months ahead). Parks with lodging areas make very nice choices, with food services, perhaps swimming or fishing, a relaxing and beautiful set-ting and, of course, plenty of rocking chairs for lengthy, relaxed fellow-ship. The attraction of the meeting place is a good motivation for getting people there. It's also important to do some advance calendar work and select a time when you're certain that loved ones are able to attend.

Work with the most organized individual in your family—the one who always seems to put plans together well—and get your family re-union on the calendar. How big do you want it to be? It could be rela-tively small, with just your children and grandchildren, or it could be a bit larger. Naturally, if your desire is to spend more regular and meaningful quality time with your grandchildren, I would assume you would opt for a smaller gathering.

If you plan well, and everyone has a good time (and it's highly likely they will, of course), then this meeting can easily become an annual tradition. Reunions can serve as a wonderful glue to hold together busy, wandering families. The years go by too quickly, and it's easy to get into a rhythm of simply sending and receiving Christmas cards; and sometimes you lose track entirely. A reunion is a terrific way to keep that from happening.

## Meaningful Moments

A less structured way of keeping in touch is to be very intentional about designing the time you spend with your grandchildren. Using the example of reunions, let's imagine that your three grandchildren are in attendance, having traveled with their parents from 400 miles away. Do something more memorable and meaningful than talking to them on the porch while rocking in chairs. You might find a nature path and take them on a hike, talking about some of the trees and plants you see. You might take them fishing or have a special picnic with no one else present but you and the children.

As they grow up, children remember the moments that really stood out for them—activities that caught their interest in some way. A child will always recall taking that nature walk with Granddad or having the special picnic over by the gazebo with Grandma. If you don't have much time, make every moment count.

The most traditional "moment" of all—the holiday season from late November until New Year's Day—is a time when grandparents are more likely to see their grandchildren than any other time. Maximize that time, and be certain that all the right positive messages are sent. Sometimes stress, anxiety and family disputes can put a damper on times that should linger positively in a child's memory for life.

## Availability

Time and money are advantages most grandparents possess. If you are retired and have at least a moderate amount of savings, you can be flexible and available for travel and planning. Use your savings to support your children's efforts to come see you. If they can't afford an airplane ticket, there's nothing wrong with a father saying, "Son, I know you're saving your money right now, paying a mortgage on that home and raising those beautiful children. I want to make a gift of your travel expenses to come see us for a week during the summer. Don't give it a second thought, because that's what our money is for. We choose to spend it on things that count; and nothing counts more for us than you and our grandchildren."

## "COME AND SEE US!"

Jack and Barbara took one other step to be the best grandparents they knew how to be. They arranged for extended visits with Little Jack.

The elementary school years are a very special window of time for children and their grandparents. If they're any younger, it's difficult for them to be away from parents; and once they reach high school, they become busy with so many activities during the summertime—friends, summer jobs, camps, sports. But when they reach the vicinity of ages 9 to 12, you may have a wonderful opportunity to spend time with them for an extended vacation that neither of you will ever forget.

Invite them to come see you for a week, or two or three weeks, or whatever period of time is a good fit for both of you. Your adult child, as a parent, may be very favorable—this idea provides a "vacation" for the parents too. Mom and Dad may leap at the chance to have a free week without the children and their activities.

Jack and Barbara were delighted to have Vince and Jane home on missionary furlough for several months during the spring. During their visit, Barbara asked, "Is it at all possible that Little Jack could stay with us for a little while after you leave? We would take care of his airfare, of course, and make all those arrangements. We would love to have Little Jack to ourselves for a few weeks and get to know him as well as we can during that time. We'll do a lot of fun things together. What do you think?"

Vince and Jane had to think about it, due to some of the issues of international travel. But in the end, they agreed that it was a wonderful idea. They knew it would be an experience their child would never forget, especially since most of his time was now spent in Brazil rather than in his home country. This would be a good thing.

As Little Jack grew older, he had continued to receive email letters, handwritten correspondence, wonderful surprise package, audio recordings and even videos of his grandparents. Those were all wonderful keepsakes, most of which he would possess and cherish for the rest of his life. But most precious of all was the memory of the June he spent in the home of his grandparents: waking in the guest bedroom each morning, having bacon and eggs fixed by his grandfather in his special way, sitting on the porch playing with the dog while his grandmother knitted, telling his new friends in the neighborhood about life in Brazil. What a nourishing experience for any child!

Grandparents can add a deep and healthy dimension to the life of a child. They are a touchpoint to an older time and to different ways of doing things. They give a child perspective about other age groups and households. And they provide a special brand of love that no one but grandparents can ever provide. I wish all grandparents could live right down the street from the children they have raised and sent out into the world. But it's very rare when that happens today. Therefore, we need to be the most effective and loving long-distance grandparents we can be.

Jack and Barbara made an impressive impact from a hemisphere and a continent away. If you're facing a number of miles away from your children and grandchildren, there's no reason that you can't do just as well.

# 4

# Parenting Your Own Grandchildren

Flo Baxter may be the most popular member of her church. People love to say that the doors could not open there without her, because she is at the center of every church activity. When an unfamiliar face enters the sanctuary, Flo is always the first person to walk up, offer a warm smile and introduce herself.

Flo throws herself into every activity with the energy of a woman 20 years younger. She happens to be 60, but her favorite expression is, "Getting old is all in the mind. Keep a young spirit and you'll have a young body."

Therefore, it didn't go unnoticed when she missed church one Sunday morning. Claire and Barbara, two of her close friends, were on the phone that afternoon to find out if all was well.

"Just took the morning off," Flo assured them. "Don't worry about me. I needed a day just to rest and recuperate, but I'll be back next week—with bells on!"

And, indeed, she was right back in her familiar pew the following Sunday. But Claire and Barbara agreed that Flo didn't look quite herself. A little bit of the spring had gone out of her step. After the service, when some of the women often lingered to chat, Flo made an excuse and headed promptly home. Her friends began to believe there was something more to the story.

During the following week, Madge Simmons, another church member, saw Flo at a fast-food restaurant. Flo was sitting in a booth with her two grandsons. Madge walked by and said hello; Flo smiled back cordially. But she seemed to have her hands full with the two small children, who were making a mess of their dinner. The younger one, about three years old, wouldn't remain in his seat. He wanted to wander everywhere and explore everything. The five-year-old was busy talking, including loudly interrupting when Flo tried to speak to Madge—who finally gave up with a sheepish smile and a good-bye wave. No wonder Flo was tired.

Poor Flo knew that people were talking, and she offered her friends an explanation. Her daughter Kim had moved back home, she said, with both children.

Kim and her husband were separated, and no one was certain how it was all going to work out. At first, it wasn't even clear how long Kim and the boys would be staying with G-Maw (the boys' name for their grandmother). Maybe Flo's daughter would cool down and move back home—or maybe not. Kim was dealing with a great deal of anger, because she had found out about her husband's extramarital affair.

Meanwhile, Flo was unprepared for (and a little embarrassed by) the whole thing. She didn't want to make a public news item out of this development; that would be "airing out our dirty laundry." Everyone knew how proud she was of her daughter, her son-in-law and especially those two beautiful children. They understood what a crisis this was for Flo, as much as for her daughter and grandkids.

Now, two weeks having passed, Kim was pretty certain that a divorce was pending. She hadn't been working before she left her husband, but now she took a job in a clothing store over at the Galleria shopping center. She was furious with her husband, Gary, and she didn't want to take a penny from him. So now she was rising early, going to work and thanking her mother ("Mama is an absolute saint!") for watching the kids during the day.

Flo, of course, felt that powerful maternal energy coming back to life within her. At first, the extra strength came from her outrage over

Gary's unfaithfulness. How could he have fooled everyone for these six years? She had loved Gary as her son-in-law, and therefore she had her own measure of anger and grief.

"You're better off without that . . . that *snake*," she said. "Mama will take care of everything. Just let me love on those two boys. Everything is going to be fine!" Flo was one of those people: in times of crisis, she was at her very best.

Unfortunately, this was a bigger crisis than the usual ones. She had no idea what was ahead for her.

## IN TOO DEEP

Flo had completely forgotten what it was like to be on the alert 16 hours a day for little ones and their needs. She might have to scoot across the room to place a lamp out of little Matthew's reach, for example. Both boys seemed to need a glass of milk, a cookie or something else every five minutes. And the *noise!* Had her children ever been this loud?

Kim came home every night at six, clearly exhausted from a day of walking the retail floor and helping customers. She tried to take over with the kids, but Flo was worried about her daughter. Kim was carrying the emotional pain from the breakup of her marriage; she was living somewhere that wasn't ideal for the needs of her two children and herself; she was adjusting to a completely new lifestyle that included the daily work grind.

So Flo had a tendency to say, "Don't worry about it! I'll get up and handle that." And when, say, Sean, the five-year-old, climbed out of bed and turned the television up to full volume at five in the morning, it would be Flo who leaped from the bed, scolded Sean and persuaded him to return to the bedroom until a decent hour.

Sean was a kindergartener, so Flo had to buckle both children into child's safety seats and take the older boy to his school each morning.

This was a scheduling impossibility for Kim. Then, early in the afternoon, she and three-year-old Matthew would pick up Sean and bring him back home. On the first afternoon at the new school, Flo had taken them both for ice cream afterward. Now they begged, pleaded and whined about another ice cream run every single day at pickup time. Flo had forgotten how to anticipate little things like that.

She would have expected to collapse into slumber every night after these exertions, but somehow it didn't work that way. She felt tensed up late at night, and then her thoughts would return to Kim and her needs. Flo continued to worry about her daughter, about her grandsons having no father and about all kinds of other issues that came into her mind late at night. She wasn't sleeping well, but the alarm clock would sound early the next morning just the same.

Flo needed help. But how could she ask for it, when it seemed to her that Kim's problems were so much bigger? Flo was a sacrificial parent who understood her role as one who carried the burden at all times.

Besides, who was there in the world that could help her?

## THE SECOND TIME AROUND

Our last major census, in the year 2000, told us that our country contains nearly 2.5 million households with children being raised by their grandparents. At the same time, 57 percent of the grandparents known to be raising their grandchildren are still in the work force.

Of course, several years after that census, the numbers can only be greater. We need to admit that our generation is experiencing something of a parenting crisis. That is, the current population of mothers and fathers is struggling to meet the requirements for successfully raising boys and girls. When all else fails, where do they turn? To their parents. In one way, these statistics honor the past work of those whose children are now grown. In another way, it's a wake-up call: We're going right back to work! Our children are crying out for help in loving and guiding the little ones who seem to require more nurture than they, the birth parents, can supply.

My own circle of friends has demonstrated to me just how urgent a point I'm about to make. It is the truth that people today will not care for their own needs.

Flo, I'm afraid, is an example of this. In times of need, she is one of those whirlwind people who seem to be everywhere at once. She is out front on church service projects; she visits hospitals; and she lives out the values of the Christian gospel, always placing others before herself. As admirable as it is, she won't be around very long to do any of it if she doesn't, at some point, look to her own basic needs. That will be my basic focus in this chapter. During the next few chapters that follow it, we will focus on the children themselves, and we'll learn the most important aspects of parenting them from the position of a grandparent.

For now, I humbly request that you view this particular chapter with special urgency. In the course of this book, we'll certainly get to the topics that intrigue you most. We've already talked about relating to your adult children. We'll also talk about your grandchildren and the cultural world that is shaping them. But at this moment, it's time to think seriously about *you*—not in a selfish way but as a matter of practicality. This is about survival skills, if you will. God loves each of us deeply. He has taught us that our bodies are His holy temple and that we are expected to care for ourselves accordingly.

As I write these words, I think about some of the best friends of my life, now departed. How I wish I had said these words to them. (In some cases, I actually did.) They were so caught up with the task of caring for others, or pursuing their goals, that they neglected their own health. All of them knew the importance of self-care. They spent countless hours preaching it to their children and their friends. There are simply too many people who never get around to taking their own advice. As it is said, "Physician, heal thyself"—but the truth is that doctors often smoke, eat the wrong foods and get too little exercise.

Our concern here is about the stresses and danger that accompany your physical, emotional and mental involvement in parenting your grandchildren. We're talking about living in the same home and doing everything a mother or father would do. If you find yourself in that situation, face the fact that it represents a radical change in life for you. Any dramatic change induces a great deal of physical and emotional stress, and that can be terribly taxing to your physical, mental and emotional health.

Therefore, you need to contemplate your own needs before the toll is paid. In a best-case scenario, with someone like Flo who is in excellent physical shape for her age, the task of an abrupt return to parenting is going to be incredibly fatiguing. But most of us don't live in best-case scenarios. The reality is that more of us than ever struggle with high blood pressure, depression, obesity or some combination of personal challenges. According to the Centers for Disease Control, half of us use at least one prescription medication; one in six of us use at least three.[1] Use of antidepressants is skyrocketing.

You need to take a realistic inventory of your present health. Your own concerns and anxieties come with you to the sudden need that your adult child has brought. Those issues will not cooperate with you by taking a sabbatical, no matter how much you may need them to do so. Even if you shove them to the back of your mind, they will still weigh upon you and do their damage.

Loving your family requires you to take care of yourself. The Bible teaches us to love others as we would love ourselves, and that teaching implies that we love ourselves first. That means caring completely and thoughtfully for your own needs. It is not going to happen all of its own accord, as much as we might wish for such a convenient arrangement. The Lord will provide for you, but you must do your part.

## Heart, Soul and Strength

Let's think of who we are from a holistic perspective. Each of us is a unified person, but we think in terms of body, mind, emotions and spirit. As we care for ourselves, we must include all the facets of our identity.

The body is a good place to start. The requirements for personal care increase as we age. We need regular sleep, the right foods and careful monitoring for certain medical challenges. We also need to acknowledge that we are, indeed, growing older. I hope that's not a problem for you! Can you begin by agreeing that you're less youthful than you were yesterday, and even less so than you were 10 years ago? That's a start.

Let's consider your diet. When I look over the studies of what Americans eat these days, I'm horrified. In the past, we ate a far more balanced diet with vegetables, fruit, whole grain and healthy protein. I find that even those in my age group are prone to eat too much fast food. If there are grandchildren in your house, you're likely to realize the need for well-balanced meals (but don't forget that you need them as much as the youngsters). The typical diet these days is loaded with fats and is heavily salted—enemies not only to the waistline but to a healthy blood pressure.

During the last 25 years, according to the *Journal of the American Medical Association,* twice as many adults are obese; three times as many children are overweight.[2] As our generation continues to reach retirement age, lifestyles will become more sedentary, and obesity will become even more prevalent.

I would recommend making an appointment with your doctor, getting a complete physical examination and having him or her recommend a diet ideally geared to your current condition. Take that recommendation seriously, based on the right foods served in the right proportions.

Now, are you getting enough exercise? I don't mean walking to the mailbox once a day, or walking across the parking lot at the grocery store. I'm talking about a regular and appropriately strenuous exercise regimen, at least twice a week. Again, listen carefully to your doctor. You can get good exercise by walking through your neighborhood or by moving about in a swimming pool. Exercise bikes and elliptical trainer machines can provide wonderful contributions to your routine. Some larger churches have health and wellness centers, generally catering to seniors and with a variety of excellent programs and opportunities. You can also enjoy an affordable membership at your local YMCA.

The benefits of exercise and appropriate diet go far beyond the physical improvements. You will feel better, more energetic, more alert and less stressed. Here's one enthusiastic suggestion: What about exercising with your adult child? Not only will it be beneficial for both of you physically, but it will also provide a wonderful time to talk about all the challenges of the present, as well as your strategies for helping the children. It works like a tonic on personal relationships. As we perspire together, we can aspire together, and the tensions in our relationship seem to melt away.

Rest is another consideration. Think about Flo, who went to bed each night physically exhausted yet unable to sleep. Have you ever encountered that problem? Sleeplessness can come with excessive anxiety or depression. Another benefit of physical exercise is that it will tire your body and dissolve a considerable portion of your stress. As a result, you'll sleep better. Every study shows that the tendency of aging people to struggle with sleep is a result of poor attention to health.

Let me give you some tips for better sleep. First, avoid beverages with caffeine after noon. Second, become a creature of habit. Go to bed and rise at consistent times each day so that your body knows what to expect on a regular basis; it will fall in line much more cooperatively that way. Third, avoid mental stimulation in the evening. Do you watch television late at night? What kind of program? As you prepare to rest, it's a wonderful idea to take the advice of the apostle Paul's words in Philippians:

Finally, brothers, whatever is true, whatever is noble, whatever is right, whatever is pure, whatever is lovely, whatever is admirable—if anything is excellent or praiseworthy—think about such things. . . . And the God of peace will be with you (Phil. 4:8-9).

Let your mind be at peace in the waning moments of the day. Talk to God, resist worrying and consider a warm bath. If you still find yourself lying awake, don't toss and turn in bed; your anxiety over the issue will only make things worse. Turn on the lights and read quietly until you feel drowsy. Don't forget: If you've gotten good, healthy exercise during the day, you're more likely to sleep well at night.

Think about the practical steps that we've discussed in this section. Imagine what your life would feel like if you ate right, exercised sufficiently and slept eight hours of quality sleep each night. You would have already taken the most important steps toward being capable of handling the challenges of caring for grandchildren. Even at your best, the task will not be easy. But as a minimum requirement, before you ever begin, you need to be certain that you are caring for your own physical needs and that your body is in optimal condition for the challenges you're going to face.

## Nothing More than Feelings

When life takes a turn, we are thrown into turmoil. The body's physical reaction to change is what we call *stress*. The greatest manifestations, however, aren't in the body but in the mind. Flo uncharacteristically told her daughter, referring to her son-in-law, "Don't worry about that snake!" She's not usually an angry person, but she's very protective of her daughter. Over a period of several days, she felt so many emotions: anger, panic, denial, grief, and even irrational optimism. Each feeling would give way to another one—and who wants to continue riding on that kind of roller coaster? We simply wear out emotionally.

Flo's situation illustrates another common occurrence. Her daughter is the obvious "victim" of the situation, with a cheating husband, a damaged marriage and a completely disrupted life. In the aftermath, people are most likely to minister to Kim and overlook her mother, Flo, who might be just as troubled. Parents like Flo suffer deeply when their children are in distress. You know this, no doubt, from your own experience. Most of us would put our children's welfare before our own every time. We would gladly take the blows in their place, but we simply cannot. As a matter of fact, we can't do a thing in the world to keep our loved ones from hurting.

When they hurt, we hurt—but our suffering is a bit more silent, and we receive less support.

Trying to simply buck up and be emotionally strong isn't effective. As a matter of fact, it is precisely the opposite; emotions cannot be swept under the carpet without creating future turmoil. We need to admit that we're hurting; we need to talk about it to those who will have compassion; and we need to decide that our happiness will not be determined by the desirability of our circumstances. We can't change the situation, but we can control how we respond to it.

Be honest about your emotions. How are you feeling? Angry? At whom are you angry? Why? What other emotions are you feeling? Sadness? Worry? It helps to talk it over with a caring friend or, of course, a loving spouse. During trying times, everyone needs at least one strong supporter upon whom to lean. Ask your best friend or your spouse to look out for you, to be ready to listen and to help when help is needed. You'll feel much less alone, and you'll be far more able to manage your emotions as they take that roller-coaster ride.

Reserve some time just for yourself too. Get away somewhere to relax, somewhere you can turn off the phone and simply rest and recharge. At home, have a place of refuge—work in the garden, take a walk or go to some private nook—where everyone must give you peace, at least for 30 minutes or an hour.

Monitor your personal anger, referring to this book's special chapter on that topic. Learn to express your specific frustrations verbally and pleasantly. You need to manage your anger and express it in words; otherwise it will begin to disrupt your life and your emotions in more damaging ways.

When the stress of dealing with youngsters begins to wear on you, stop and step back. Take a walk or retreat to your private place for a few minutes if it's practical to do so. If not, perhaps you can call a good friend to watch the kids for a few moments while you take a break. Practice slow, deep breathing to normalize your heart rate and respiration. Use positive self-talk with statements such as, "I'm having a hard time, but that's normal for this situation. God gave me the strength I have and friends who love me. Through His grace, I can make it through today. Tomorrow I'll worry about that day. I'm not going to react negatively because of negative feelings. I am going to let this challenge make me a better person."

If you need such medication as an antidepressant, allow a doctor to make that prescription. If you have that chemical need, it is as legitimate as a diabetic's need for insulin; there is nothing "un-Christian" about the use of modern medicine.

At the same time, it goes without saying that you should watch out for the emotional needs of your adult child; but you're more likely to do this on your own without my nagging you!

## GETTING INTO THE SPIRIT OF THINGS

How about your spiritual needs? Yes, they're important too, and they need to be addressed directly.

Over the years, I've watched many families deal with difficult situations. I can certainly tell you that those with a spiritually grounded understanding of life have prevailed much more successfully. There are some who believe this life is all there is, and its circumstances occur randomly and without deeper meaning. I can't imagine facing life with that outlook, but I know that many people do. On the other hand, there are people who believe that nothing occurs without a reason, no matter how unfortunate the event may seem. They believe that God watches over us and it is not His doing or His desire when bad things happen, and He grieves along with us.

Some people shake their fist at heaven when life goes wrong; others open that hand and lift it toward God in supplication. They find that He comforts and strengthens us according to our needs. I hope that you won't forget your God while coping with the challenges of parenting a grandchild. He is the greatest possible supplier of all that we may need. You might memorize this comforting passage, again from the letter to the Philippians:

> Do not be anxious about anything, but in everything, by prayer and petition, with thanksgiving, present your requests to God. And the peace of God, which transcends all understanding, will guard your hearts and your minds in Christ Jesus (Phil. 4:6-7).

I hope you've discovered, as I have, that God keeps that promise. His peace transcends all understanding, and particularly any attempt by me to describe it. Be vigilant in prayer and study of the Scriptures. Ask specifically for His wisdom and strength in dealing with children as well as with your adult son or daughter. And finally, reach out to your fellow church members and let them know about your emotional and spiritual needs. One of the greatest gifts God has given us is the gift of a community to surround and support us in our needs.

In the next section, we'll explore the importance of a community in this situation of parenting or helping to parent your grandchildren.

## CARE FROM YOUR COMMUNITY

Flo made the classic mistake. As soon as her great challenge material-
ized, she cut herself off from the world, intending to face the fire alone.

Why do we do that? Perhaps we don't want to burden others. Perhaps we're a little embarrassed or taken off guard, and we simply don't
think about asking for help. For Flo, it might have been a little of all
three reasons. Whatever the case, we should send up the distress signal
sooner rather than later. We will want to know that people are aware of
what has happened, are praying for us and are already thinking of ways
they can help us in crisis.

As you know, Flo is a beloved member of her church. As a matter of
fact, over the years, she has served nearly every other member there in
one way or another. In some cases, she made a significant difference in
their own crises. How do you think they would respond in hearing that
she is now the one in need? Surely they would want to rush to her aid.
But what could they do?

For one thing, they could frequently lend a hand to help with the
children. Madge Simmons was the friend who spotted Flo and the
grandchildren at a fast-food restaurant, for example. It might just as
well have been Madge who took the children to dinner while Flo took
advantage of an hour to herself. It might be some other friend who
could take the children for an afternoon and allow Flo to go grocery
shopping, make a trip to the pharmacy or whatever else she needed to
do—without having to cope with children at the same time.

Our churches are filled with retired folks who love children and often have time on their hands. Isn't it a small tragedy that some of us
struggle with our grandchildren alone while there is an available army of
supporters who would be delighted to have an hour or two in the presence of children? (Note: Anyone who is allowed to be near your grandchildren, of course, should be someone who has been in your community

or church for years, and you know the person extremely well.)

Everyone needs to give and to receive love, and there are empty nesters in your group of friends who would leap at such an opportunity. If you're parenting your grandchildren, and you don't live on a tiny island, there's no reason that you must be isolated by your task. Look around you. Who is there to help you?

## PASSING INSPECTION

Every year I take my car to be inspected for its vehicle emissions. There are certain requirements that must be fulfilled, a checklist that must be completed. If every checkbox isn't checked, my car won't be allowed on the road.

I'm being very serious when I suggest that we as grandparents need to inspect ourselves much more thoroughly than our cars are examined. At least no one will slap a sticker on your forehead!

Before you take on the task of resuming the parenthood of younger children, you need to inspect yourself mentally, spiritually, emotionally and physically. I've saved this point for last because it is the most important of all.

Your tendency is to say, "It's not a choice. My child has come to me in need, and I must do something! I have to take on these children, because who else will do so?"

Please consider the possibility that if you take that attitude, and if it turns out that you can't handle all the demands of the task, things will be much worse than they are now, not better. Your adult child will not only have the problem of children who need supervision, but he or she will also have the problem of a parent who suddenly needs care as well.

Looking once again at Flo's situation, of course she had to take in her daughter and grandchildren when they appeared on the doorstep. But once everyone had a place to sleep, and once the dust had settled for the time being, she needed some time to sort things out and decide what *all* her options might be.

Consider these questions if you are ever in Flo's position: Is your home the only place that is available? Are you the only person who can help? There are nearly always more options than there may seem to be in the first blush of a crisis. Perhaps there can be a compromise of some kind. Perhaps one child can stay in one home, the other in another home. Perhaps your adult child has friends who can provide support. Think creatively and thoroughly, because you are being asked to adopt the most challenging task possible.

It's always possible to say no, even to our own children, if we truly believe that we can't physically handle the task. That would not be a selfish response, but the very opposite; it would be more loving and more beneficial for the children, the parents, and you, if you're only going to buckle later under too heavy a burden. We all have our limits, and our age is a key factor affecting those limits.

Your grandchildren will require unconditional love and security. They'll need to be supervised by an adult who can keep a positive attitude and a premium level of energy, and who will have the physical space and the financial resources to fulfill every parenting need that arises. You were successful as a parent years ago, but you're not the same person now, and the needs of these children will be different. Therefore, consider all these things. If you have to say no, then do so in a gentle and loving way, with an explanation of why the loving thing to do is to avoid collapsing over a load that you can't bear—if that happened, the children would take the fall.

You can see now why I felt you needed to read this chapter. We focus outward on the people who need us; but one of those people is *inside*, rather than out. If you don't care for yourself, no one else will.

If you *do* decide that you can be an effective parent to your grandchildren, please reread the chapter you've just completed. Continue to care for your physical, emotional and spiritual needs. As for the needs of your children, we'll begin to explore those in the next few chapters.

**Notes**

1. "Prescription Drug Use in the Past Month by Sex, Age, Race and Hispanic Origin: United States, 1988-1994 and 1999-2002," *Health, United States, 2007,* National Center for Health Statistics, Table 96. http://www.cdc.gov/nchs/fastats/drugs.htm (accessed April 2007).

2. "Obesity and Other Diet and Inactivity Related Diseases: National Impact, Costs and Solutions," National Alliance for Nutrition and Activity (NANA), 2005. http://www.cspinet.org/nutritionpolicy/NANA_advocates_national_policies.pdf (accessed April 2007).

# 5

*·—∞—·*

# The Love Your Grandchild Must Have

# Must Have

Hank glances thoughtfully over his newspaper. He studies the little girl sitting several feet away as she stares vacantly at a television screen where a frenetic cartoon is playing. Hank wonders what thoughts and feelings might be going on inside that little head.

Hank is a grandfather, working overtime to understand a six-year-old's world. It's not the same as a five-year-old's world, or a four-year-old's. Children seem to change and grow remarkably between every visit. They soak in the world with those wide eyes, hear every word that is said and rapidly climb that ladder of knowledge and confidence. It all happens too fast, Hank reflects. We hardly have time to enjoy them at one age before they're already in a headlong rush toward the next.

Just a few minutes ago, Ginny, his granddaughter, peeked around his newspaper. "Boo!" she shouted, her little hands creating pretend-antlers over her head. Hank happened to be in the middle of a very compelling article about the NFL playoff matchups. He had a nearly irresistible urge to hang on and finish the sentence he was reading.

But Hank, a good sport and a loving grandfather, "booed" right back. Ginny covered her mouth and giggled. Talk about irresistible. Hank gathered her in and sat her on his lap. It wouldn't be long before she'd be too old for laps and games of "Boo!"

"Guess what?" whispered Hank into Ginny's ear, as if bearing a dark secret.

"What?" Ginny returned quickly, her eyes glowing in curiosity and fun.

"I've got your nose," Hank whispered. He displayed his two hands, clasped together to hold some secret inside.

"My nose isn't in there!" cried Ginny triumphantly. "It's right here on my face!"

"Can't be," disagreed Hank, shaking his head. "I've got it right in here."

"Uh *uh*," said Ginny emphatically. She rubbed her nose into his cheek. "See?" she said. "Dat's my *dose!*"

Hank donned a deeply confused face. "Then whose nose is this in my hands?"

"You *don't—got—*a nose!" All of this was part of a familiar script, each line a part of the tradition since Ginny was three. Just about now, she would begin to get bored with it; that made Hank a little sad.

"Do too!" insisted Hank, clutching his cupped hands to his chest. Ginny laughed, as always, and tried to separate his hands to reveal the deception. Her G-Daddy was supposed to surrender, open his hands and feign anger at being found out—which would send Ginny into gales of laughter, intensified by a few good tickles to the belly by G-Daddy.

For some reason, this time Hank wouldn't open his hands. Maybe he was just curious to see how a six-year-old Ginny would respond. Maybe it was a touch of that competitive nature that so many males have, even when playing with children. He merely tightened his grip.

Ginny looked up at him, surprised, then back at his hands, redoubling her efforts to pry them open. They wouldn't budge.

She looked at him again, this time impatiently; he met her glance with nothing more than raised eyebrows.

*"G-Daddy! You're not playing right!"* Tears rushed out as Ginny pushed away from her grandfather's lap. Storming from the room, she called for her G-Mommy to report Hank's wicked antics.

Hank sighed and shook his head, a bit startled. So much for trying to understand children. He lifted his newspaper and resumed reading.

## THE GREATEST NEED OF ALL

Who are these little strangers who visit our home?

It is my experience that those of us who are old enough to be grandparents are fascinated by children. Our world, after all, is a largely adult one by that time. Most of our friends are our age, and they, too, have empty nests.

Then come our children, bringing their own children. Little ones seem so noisy! We forget that we were once accustomed to the sound volume and the hectic pace of youngsters. There was a time when we patiently followed our toddlers around the room, removing anything inappropriate from their reach and straightening out the rugs and furniture they had disturbed. For years, we built our lives around our children.

Then, after a time, the idea of children almost seemed new again. These times are so different: the kids watch a different manner of television show, play with a different manner of toys and—well, they have different manners, don't they?

The fact is that their basic needs have not changed at all. Only the background has changed, and it is that cultural background and its influences that we must heed. At the same time, we simply need to remember that today's children need what they have always needed. I believe that there are four foundational requirements for all children. To echo the words of 1 Corinthians 13, "the greatest of these is love."

We love our grandchildren. Their parents love them too. The question before us is whether the children *fully receive* the love that is there. The world throws into place many obstacles that can keep children from feeling the love they must have. Parents can get distracted by their careers, the challenges of their marriage or by some other personal struggle. A child stands in the confusion and wonders, *Where is the place for me? What will happen to me? Am I loved?*

It is precisely here that I believe the grandparent can make a powerful and permanent contribution to the wellbeing of that child. It is the grandmother and/or the grandfather who stands behind the parent and the child with a heart full of love for both of them. The grandparent has the perspective of years and, hopefully, the time and leisure to provide extra love for the child just when that child really needs it. There is no way to over-love a child; none of us, for that matter, can ever receive too much genuine love. Children need so much of it, and parents can't always provide it successfully or consistently enough.

The other basic needs of a child, in my estimation, are discipline, security and guidance in managing anger. Try to imagine how we could possibly provide any of these needs if we didn't meet the most basic need of all. If a child feels unloved, that child will be cut off from parents or grandparents, or anyone else. As you look at your grandchild, I want you to always be asking yourself these questions: Does this child feel profoundly, unconditionally loved? When and how can I express my love and support for this child again?

Expressing love must be done consistently, and it must continue at every age, whether that child is a toddler, a teenager or a twentysomething. In this chapter, we'll find out why so many children today feel unloved. I'll help you understand how younger children understand love (for we must communicate in their language if we want to communicate successfully). We'll also explore the basic methods at our disposal for giving love to our grandchildren.

## What We Say, How They Hear

Sydney J. Harris said, "Love that is not expressed in loving action does not really exist, just as talent that does not express itself in creative works does not exist; neither of these is a state of mind or feeling, but an activity, or it is a myth."[1] Love is primarily active, something that must be experienced. That's true for all of us. But it is truer for children than we can begin to imagine. Children do not think conceptually, as adults do. They don't grasp love as an abstract idea; they grasp it as a personal experience.

Let's return to Hank, reader of the sports page. Perhaps last week his wife passed through the room and said, "Hank, do you love me?"

He might have grunted, "Of course I do," being immersed as he was in an article about the New England Patriots.

She might have asked, "Are you sure?"

He might have replied, sensibly enough: "Haven't I honored our marriage for 30 years? Have I ever cheated on you or lied to you?"

She would have to agree that the answer was no. But love is more than a statement, isn't it? It's something we need to see and feel and experience—and yes, hear—even after 30 years. It's not a matter for general assumption. Love needs regular illustration.

If we, as verbally oriented adults—people who can grasp abstract ideas—need tangible assurance, how much more is it true for children, who are behavioral in orientation? How do we teach a child any lesson? We show. We use pictures and touch and repetition. Children experience the world through what they see, hear and touch with their hands.

Mommy and Daddy might insist that they tell their child "I love you" at least once or twice a day. To them, the words equal a powerful statement of love. And those three words do have meaning for the child—just not as fully and powerfully as we think.

Consider it this way. How would you define love for your child or grandchild? You could write a lengthy paragraph explaining all the depth of your love, your willingness to sacrifice your own comfort for that person, the way you value him or her above others, and so on. But a child doesn't have that depth of experience or understanding.

The child understands basically and behaviorally.

As a matter of fact, that child has also heard Mommy and Daddy say that they "love" lasagna, several particular TV shows and the shirt the child is wearing today.

Therefore, when you say, "I love you," to your grandchild, what goes through *your* mind is the complex definition of love that is the product of your life and thought—something like the definition two paragraphs above. What the child *hears* is three simple words that simply say, "I like you very much, as I do certain foods and colors." See? You've attempted to give a treasure's worth of love, but the whole gift was not received. Lost in translation, as they say.

As time goes on, of course, this will change. You can talk to a teenager in abstract terms and your message will translate more accurately. With a smaller child, however, we must learn to express our love in a more appropriate "language." We must demonstrate our love in a visible, memorable manner.

In doing so, not only are we nurturing them in a very healthy way, but we are also teaching them to show love themselves. As a counselor, I find that adults who struggle to show their feelings are people who have come from families that failed to express emotions in a healthy way. You don't want your grandchild to bottle up her feelings in a way that will ultimately impact her own children someday.

Now is the time for us to model a loving transparency with our emotions. And to do that, you really need to set a tone, both for your grandchild and for her parents. Let's learn how to create that setting.

## THE RIGHT ENVIRONMENT

It's always important to set the mood, isn't it?

In the sanctuary of a church, for example, you want to create an environment of worship. You wouldn't walk into the back of the auditorium and shout a raucous hello to a friend sitting on the front pew.

We set the mood for our holidays. We want Christmas to *feel* like Christmas, so we decorate our homes. As a matter of fact, we want it to feel like "Christmases long, long ago," so we use many of the same decorations, in much the same way. We gather our family and hope to feel that "Christmas spirit," which is largely a state of mind, a mood we set.

If we want to create a household of love, we also need to do a little work on the setting and the atmosphere—and the atmosphere we want is one of unconditional love.

I trust that you understand that phrase "unconditional love," but allow me to say a little more about it. We speak of unconditional love, but isn't genuine love unconditional simply by definition? Paul the apostle never used the word "unconditional," but his definition of love, found in 1 Corinthians 13, gives a powerful picture of a love that has no strings attached, a love that is not a contract but a commitment. What sets that love apart is the amazing concept known as *grace.*

The love of Christ is different and above every other love in the following way: It functions completely apart from anyone being worthy of it. Jesus loved and forgave the people who beat Him, mocked Him and drove nails into His hands before leaving Him to die on a cross. He thus made a demonstration of that love that no one could ever deny. We might say that any *conditional* form of love is not love at all, but merely a contractual agreement: *I will treat you well if you meet my demands.* It took Jesus to show us real love.

Better yet, Jesus is not the only one who can manifest that love. We are taught by the Bible that, through God's power, we can now embrace people with the love that He has for us. Paul tells us that this brand of love "always protects, always trusts, always hopes, always perseveres. Love never fails" (1 Cor. 13:7-8). Take the word "love" in those two verses and substitute "grandparents." Your grandchild would be able to say this:

My grandparents always protect me, always trust me, always hope for my best, always persevere in putting up with me. They never fail me.

Those words should be your credo as a grandparent. They should be written upon your heart so that your every contact with your grandchildren is guided by them.

## HOW DO THEY SEE YOUR HOME?

We teach children that good behavior brings a good result, and that poor behavior has consequences too. The idea that they should never absorb (but sometimes do) is that love is equally conditional—that when they misbehave, they will lose their parents' or grandparents' love. Of course they won't, but we need to help them see the truth of it.

What I want you to consider now is how we have traditionally approached the subject of grandparents and what they require. We have driven our own children to Grandmother's house, and we have told them on the way: "Listen carefully to me. You'd better be on your best behavior! None of that foolishness or you will be heavily punished, because this is Grandmother's house!"

We have dressed them up, combed their hair and threatened them within an inch of their lives if they so much as cause Grandmother an ounce of anxiety. What were we telling the children? *Grandparents have a lower level of tolerance; they won't accept children as they are.* This is not a message that should be sent.

Certainly we want grandchildren to behave. It would be wonderful to have their best deportment. But we don't want that to come from fear. John writes, "There is no fear in love. But perfect love drives out fear, because fear has to do with punishment. The one who fears is not made perfect in love" (1 John 4:18).

I'm not suggesting that you let your grandchildren run wild in your home. We can be firm and provide a guiding hand in training mature behavior, but we also want our home to be a setting of grace and unconditional love. If there ever came a time when that child could not find a safe place to turn, a sanctuary that would permit his or her full honesty, we wouldn't want our home to be the least likely choice. We would want it to be the first, after the parents', of course.

The questions we must always be asking ourselves, in good times and bad, are: What is the atmosphere in my home? How comfortable, secure and loved do my grandchildren feel? Do my grandchildren know that no matter what happens in their life, no matter what terrible mistakes they might make, they will never, ever lose my love?

To help set an atmosphere of unconditional love, I have adapted a simple set of propositions that I used as a parent. You might want to reflect on these truths every time you prepare to spend time with your grandchildren:

1. Our grandchildren are, after all, children.
2. Therefore they will tend to be childish.
3. Childishness annoys grandparents.
4. Our love helps them move beyond childishness to maturity.
5. Conditional love will create insecurity, low self-esteem and prolonged immaturity.
6. Therefore I accept co-responsibility, with their parents, for their behavior and growth.
7. Gracious love is my investment toward gracious, loving children.

If patience and nerves provide a challenge for you when your grandchildren are around, I suggest combining the words above with prayer. The only source of the love I've described is in God Himself. He will freely give you the grace you need to be tolerant yet firm. Ask God to help you imagine your grandchildren in the future, as the adults you wish them to be: self-confident and mature, warm and loving in a way that is reflective of the love they have received.

I guarantee you that God will answer that prayer.

## FILLING THE TANK

Have you ever driven a car that ran out of gas? There's nothing more frustrating. We take for granted that the automobile will carry us where we'd like to go. The fuel tank is something that is hidden from view, so we tend to disregard it. Yet it is absolutely essential for the functionality of an automobile.

Children (much like the rest of us) have emotional tanks that must be filled. They need love, acceptance and security to live and function well. At regular intervals, someone must fill that tank. You and I certainly need reassurance from time to time; we cannot live without the expression of love. But we can go a bit farther and for a longer time than children. Think of a child's tank as small, running through its "fuel" rather rapidly and needing more. Therefore, several times a day, your grandchild should receive your love in some way. A warm smile and a hug count as a trip to the emotional "filling station." A warm, encouraging word is more fuel for their tank.

There are at least three crucial effects to filling your child's tank. First, her emotional wellness is increased. She is that much healthier and more content in spirit. Second, her behavior is more likely to be positive and acceptable. So much of the misbehavior of children is a simple result of the need for that tank to be filled. A child who crosses the line of permissibility in some matter is likely saying, "Do you still love me? Are you paying attention?" Therefore, if you would like a younger child to behave more acceptably, give her the love she needs.

By the way, a teenager's behavior is more complex, but a well-loved teenager is far less likely to act rebelliously.

The third result of filling the emotional tank is that a child learns to love. Loving others is not a natural instinct; it is a behavior that must be trained through repetition and reinforcement. Your grandchild will reflect the love she has received and will either love others or fail to love them, as a result. The child who receives conditional love will love others conditionally. Therefore, please know that whenever you love your grandchild in some way, you are teaching a lesson that will last for a lifetime. "We love because [God] first loved us," wrote the apostle John (1 John 4:19). Because God loved us first, we love our children and grandchildren, and they pass on that wonderful blessing to the world for generations to come.

I know you understand the philosophy of biblical love. I'm certain it's not news to you that the best policy is to love your grandchildren unconditionally, thoroughly and frequently. But perhaps your question is *how* to do that. You'd like some practical examples of how a grandparent can fill the emotional tank of a grandchild.

Let's discuss three practical ways to apply this principle.

## THREE BRANDS OF FUEL FOR THE TANK

First, your love must be proactive. It must take the initiative rather than waiting for some obvious timing. Every day, every occasion when you are with your grandchild, you need to provide love in some way. It's an active philosophy that must be constant and consistent.

Second, be aware of how well your adult children, as the parents, fill the child's emotional love tank. Ultimately they are the ones who should be the primary love-givers. You can make a great difference in supplementing that love, filling in the blanks and showing that the child has more support than simply in the parents' home. But you need to be aware of how well those parents are making the child feel loved unconditionally and accepted, as well as how they go about doing so. Watch the parents and the children interact together. Pay attention to their patterns of affection. In this section we'll show you the three primary methods to watch for, but keep an eye out for how frequently and how well your adult child loves your grandchild.

You'll want to share the information in this chapter with your children. As a matter of fact, you may want to give them their own copies of my books written primarily for parents, such as *How to Really Love Your Child* and *How to Really Parent Your Child.* Some of the basic principles laid out in this book can be found there, applied to the particular situation of the parent.

And remember, behavior counts above anything else with children. The following "fuels" for the emotional tank are applied through your behavior and interaction with the child.

## First Fuel: The Look of Love

It's fascinating to consider how God designed our eyes to be used in the giving of love. From the very beginning of life, the eyes seek the emotional gratification needed by the soul.

Your infant grandchild's eyes will begin to focus at two to four weeks of age. The most primary image for the newborn child is a human face; the most primary part of that, in turn, are the eyes. As a baby begins to think more intelligently and gain coordination, she searches for another set of eyes. When she finds them, she "locks on" like a radar signal. Already a newborn child is trying to fill her emotional tank in the most basic, primitive form of communication, because that is all that is available at her level.

We can even see that God designed the child's eyes to make contact with her mother during breast-feeding. As she feeds physically with her mouth, she feeds emotionally with her eyes. When it comes to giving love, the eyes have it.

Hank, our grandfather from the beginning of this chapter, has learned this lesson so well that he no longer has to think about it. The first time Ginny peered around his newspaper and said, "Boo," he smiled vaguely, said, "Boo," right back, and continued reading.

That didn't work at all. Ginny said, *"Boo!"* with much more insistence. He tried looking at her momentarily, then returning to that captivating football article he was reading. Finally he came to understand that what Ginny was really doing was asking a question: "Do you still love me? Have you forgotten about me?" If the newspaper is really more important than the grandchild, the grandchild will figure that out very quickly. When it comes to the all-important question of worth, children are extremely perceptive. They will not be fooled.

Since Hank did adore his granddaughter, he learned quickly to put his newspaper down when a new game started up. There were a few times, of course, when he was in the middle of some task that would not wait. Then he could simply ask Ginny to be patient for just a second. But most of the time, he found that it was the eye contact that told Ginny, "You are more important to me than anything in the world right now."

In short, children want to see our eyes, the windows to the soul. Are you any different? I expect you've recently carried on a conversation at church or the local store and not been honored with the eye contact of your friend. How did that make you feel? What message did it send you? People pay us respect when they look into our eyes and listen carefully to what we're saying, without interruption or hurry. As a matter of fact, if you could master those two simple considerations—looking intently, listening closely—you would become one of the most popular people around!

When your grandchild is speaking to you, pull her close to you. Look into her eyes and give her your complete attention. You're not saying a word, yet you're saying everything: "You are important. You are special enough for me to stop what I'm doing so that you are the center of my universe for the time being."

Think about how much information you derive from the eyes of someone with whom you're talking. The eyes do the lead actor role; the rest of the face, of course, is the supporting cast. You can receive a full understanding of this person's emotions by reading the eyes and the face. Now, given our explanation that children are visual and behavioral, consider how so much of what you *can't* get across simply by saying, "I love you," can be communicated by your eyes and your demeanor as you pay attention to your grandchild.

Hank uses his eyes in the boo-game with Ginny. First, he has a mock startled look when she boos at him. She knows it is a playful look, and that is an "I love you." Then he gives her what is almost a conspiratorial look when he tells her the "secret" that something is in his hands. Children love being part of a secret, even a play-secret. This affords a child a certain kind of power, something children rarely have. It says again, "I love you." Then, when he refuses to open his hands for her, as the "rules" specify, we notice that he simply raises his eyebrows. Even this communicates something to Ginny, though something more aloof. This is why she feels confused and even betrayed.

Your eyes are the visible evidence of the connection between you and your grandchild. They link you together in a moment of shared understanding, the precious communication we all crave. We can say "I love you" in so many ways, simply by looking at someone!

What are some enemies of good eye contact? The television is a primary "enemy"—the thief of attention. As long as a television is playing in a room, our eyes wander toward it. We don't look at each other. If a grandchild suddenly feels lost and forgotten in a room, and wants to say something, it's tempting to answer verbally without making eye contact. A book or a rose garden or a cooking pot—anything else that has our attention can keep us from eye contact.

Again, there are some items that simply cannot wait (at times the cooking pot may be one of them) but so many things that have our attention *can* wait. There is a wonderful new innovation in television called the digital video recorder (DVR). It makes it possible to pause your television show, even during a live transmission, while someone in the room is talking. Therefore, while you're watching that intense mystery show, you need not either "shush" your grandchild or miss a key line of dialogue. You can simply touch a button and your show will wait.

We should add that this section implies nothing negative toward sight-impaired people. The point is that when we do have well-functioning eyes, those around us expect us to use them. They constitute a gift that can keep giving.

## Second Fuel: The Loving Touch

Everyone understands the need for physical contact, but, as with the eyes, we often fail to realize the power that is given to us through this opportunity.

When your grandchildren come for a visit, your first act, presumably, is to invite your grandchild to come give and receive a big hug. We do this because we recognize the power of the love message we send with a sturdy embrace.

We need to be certain, however, that we find many other opportunities to physically touch our grandchildren. The University of Miami School of Medicine's Touch Research Institute tells us that American parents lag in the frequency of touching their children. French parents, for example, touch their children more than three times more often than we do.[2] That's an important finding, in my opinion, because it reveals that we're missing one of the surest methods of filling the love tank. I would guess that even some grandfathers hug children awkwardly, because they were not embraced frequently enough earlier in life. A stiff, hasty embrace will be less effective in saying "I love you."

If grandchildren have a deficit when it comes to feeling a loving touch, here is an opportunity for grandparents to take up the slack. They will find that their grandchildren crave physical contact. The younger ones will want to sit on your lap. At any age, they'll respond positively to tousled hair, a rub on the shoulder or a kiss on the cheek at an unexpected time, "just because." It is the non-standard touch that really makes a statement to our grandchildren. It reinforces the message that love is not a reward for good behavior but an unconditional reality that is always present. Loving physical touch is so important in creating that atmosphere of grace in a grandparent's home. You may even now remember the smell of your own grandmother's perfume, and the gentle feel of her embrace. Your grandchild will forever carry that same kind of memory of you, because it will resound so positively to them. What a marvelous way to fill the emotional tank!

Since the time of the stories recorded in Genesis, parents have blessed their children via physical touch. Hebrew fathers laid their hands on the heads of their children to bestow goodness and fortune on their lives—which is precisely what touch does. In church, we often ordain someone for a task of ministry by laying hands upon their head.

Your question might well be, "How can I touch or hug or kiss without overdoing it?" You can, in fact, find many varieties of physical contact: a gentle touch on the shoulder; mussing the hair; scratching the back; even a playful poke in the ribs—you can find a variety of ways to touch your grandchild in a meaningful way.

Studies demonstrate that touch promotes not only emotional growth but physical growth as well. Prematurely born infants receiving three 15-minute periods of slow, firm massage strokes each day experienced a staggering 47 percent greater weight gain than infants not receiving this attention. The massaged children also demonstrated superior sleep, alertness and physical activity.[3]

Next question: What about teenage grandchildren? Don't they shy away from being touched? Do they still need this expression of love?

Yes, they do—just as you do. It may seem harder than ever to say "I love you," because they can seem sullen and nonverbal. It may also be more difficult to maintain eye contact. Even focused attention, the third strategy, can be pushed away by teenagers. And because teenagers are a bit physically awkward or reticent at times, they crave touch more than they realize. But if you pick your opportunities carefully, you can be very effective in giving love this way.

A light touch on the shoulder, at the right time, can communicate. Other subtle touches will make more difference than you think they do. Ecclesiastes 3:5 tells us that there is "a time to embrace and a time to refrain from embracing." Be wise about when to approach your grandchild. Don't withdraw from your teenager, because adolescents face a world of challenges. They need the love of a grandparent more than ever, even if they don't look you in the eye very well, and even if they constantly seem to have ear-buds stuck into their ears. What they want to know more than ever is this: "Do you still love me now that I've grown up, my voice is awkward and I'm not a cute child anymore?"

A warm touch says, "Yes, I do."

There is one other method for fueling the emotional tank.

## THIRD FUEL: FOCUSED ATTENTION

Our third strategy, focused attention, takes a greater sacrifice. Eye contact and physical touch are not time-intensive, but now we're talking about giving that most precious of commodities to our grandchildren.

Mark Twain said, "We are always too busy for our children; we never give them the time or interest they deserve. We lavish gifts upon them; but the most precious gift, our personal association, which means so much to them, we give grudgingly."

As I teach this concept to parents, I urge them to work on their appointment books. This is a hurried and hectic generation, and grandchildren and their parents are both too busy. What about you? More than half of you today are still in the workforce, we are told, as you become grandparents. Many others, however, are retired and may have the extra time that can make such a difference to their grandchildren. Here is yet another opportunity when grandparents can really shine.

How can you spend time with them? You could help tutor them with homework needs. You could encourage them to come by just to talk. You could spend special time alone with each grandchild once a month.

Focused time is unshared time. It means that you are with your grandchild, and he or she has your full attention. Parents are able to award this gift to their children with less frequency than in the past. If a child lives with both parents these days, both of them may be working. If that is the case with your grandchildren, why not take the opportunity to spend more time with them? When the child understands that what Grandmother and Grandfather want most is to be with them, they will know that they are profoundly loved.

I often think about Jesus and how He focused His time. He was given, in the heavenly economy of things, three years to accomplish the ministry that would change all of human history. He knew that in a matter of mere months, He would be arrested and executed. Yet notice how He used at least two of the "fuels" for filling the emotional tanks of children He didn't even know:

> People were bringing little children to Jesus to have him touch them, but the disciples rebuked them. When Jesus saw this, he was indignant. He said to them, "Let the little children come to me, and do not hinder them, for the kingdom of God belongs to such as these. I tell you the truth, anyone who will not receive

the kingdom of God like a little child will never enter it." And he took the children in his arms, put his hands on them and blessed them (Mark 10:13-16).

I think that we can accurately assume that Jesus also looked these children in the eye. He touched them, He spent the most precious time we can imagine with them and, thus, He showed again what it really means to love a child, or anyone else. Can you, as a grandparent, follow His model?

## GRANDPARENTS AND GIFTS

You may notice that I haven't suggested one method of showing love that grandparents always choose: gift-giving.

It's (almost) always good to give gifts, and there is no denying that a gift makes a very positive statement. We also know that it can be an ambiguous statement at times. Many spoiled children are given gifts without particularly feeling that there was any real love attached; sometimes the opposite message can come across—that a thing has been bought rather than love given.

The truth is that gifts, nice as they may be, are never a substitute for genuine love. They can't fill the emotional tank in the way that eye contact, touch and focused time can do. I think it's wonderful that God created love to be a free thing, something that anyone in the world can give. No one need ever spend a cent, yet he or she can give love lavishly and to overflowing.

Emotional needs, you see, require emotional solutions. The only gift you can give your grandchild that makes a difference is yourself, and that's measured not in dollars and cents but in hours and minutes, and the genuine proof that these children matter more to us than anything else. Fill their tanks and you will have the joy of seeing *their* joy.

You'll also have the contentment of knowing that you're touching a life and teaching a lifestyle.

Paul wrote, "Be very careful, then, how you live—not as unwise but as wise, making the most of every opportunity, because the days are evil" (Eph. 5:15-16). I don't know whether our own times are more evil than the ones in which he wrote. But it's safe to say that these times are pretty dark as well. Your grandchild faces tremendous challenges in this culture. It's so tempting for us to wring our hands and say, "What will they do? How will they get along?"

They will get along quite well if we give them the love they need. For then they will be emotionally secure, self-confident, driven by integrity and capable of making a positive difference so that one day, their own children can face better prospects. This is your time as a grandparent. Parenting your own children was an incredible experience, but you have more work to do. Give your grandchildren love; fill their tanks. You will leave a powerful legacy.

**Notes**
1. Sydney J. Harris, quoted in Glenn Van Ekeren, *Speaker's Sourcebook II: Quotes, Stories, & Anecdotes for Every Occasion* (Englewood Cliffs, NJ: Prentice Hall, 1994,) p. 244.
2. "Research at TMI," University of Miami School of Medicine Touch Research Institute. http://www6.miami.edu/touch-research/research.htm (accessed April 2007).
3. Ibid.

# 6

The Anger Your
Grandchild Expresses

Josh calls her Gramma. He has always adored her, and she feels the same way about him. But now he needs her help, and she has no strong idea about what to do.

Both of them sit on the sofa, watching the front door close. They listen until they hear Josh's dad's car backing out of the driveway. Josh is fumbling with his portable music player. He powers it down with his thumb and slips it into some hidden pocket of his long, droopy jacket. Maybe he's ready to talk.

"Tell Gramma what happened," she says softly.

Josh doesn't respond for a moment, then shrugs. "Mmdnno," he mumbles.

"It's the middle of the day. My guess is there's been some kind of situation at school."

"Uh huh."

"Suspended this time?"

"Mmhmm."

Gramma wonders why Josh has lost the ability to communicate in sentences and look people in the eye. He didn't used to be like this—why, he was the most appealing little boy you've ever met, before he became this sullen teenage figure seemingly overnight.

Some instinct tells Gramma not to force the issue; maybe it's just good common sense, knowing that he won't talk until he's completely ready. She picks up her knitting and sits patiently. Josh heaves a long sigh and leans back against the sofa cushions. He begins to reach for his music player but restrains himself.

*Good,* Gramma thinks to herself—*maybe he does intend to speak at some point. With Josh, who really knows?*

Suddenly he says, "I stole some money."

Gramma's heart sinks. What she wants to do is grab him by the shoulders, shake him and say, "What do you mean, you stole? Don't you remember who you are? You were raised better than that! What in blazes has gotten into you lately? You stole, when you have everything you need?"

That's what she wanted to do, but somehow she holds back. She avoids reacting and simply says, "Hmm. What did you steal?"

"Money. From some kid. Left his locker open. Chick saw me and ratted me out."

"I see."

Josh heaves another sigh.

"So what happens now?" Gramma asks.

"Mmdnno."

"Need a cola?"

"Sure." He seems to appreciate that. She catches him looking at her for just a second.

As Grandma stands at the kitchen counter and divides a can of cherry cola between two glasses, she sees a picture of Josh. He was 10 when it was taken—seems like 4 weeks ago instead of 4 years ago. What a room-brightening smile he had; it outshone the Christmas tree behind him.

Gramma used to tell everyone how perfect her grandson was: super-special, one-in-a-million, sharp as a tack, headed for the U.S. presidency—or maybe a Nobel Peace Prize, hard to decide which. She knew it was her grandparent pride talking; Josh was an ordinary boy then, delightfully appealing and just a tad mischievous.

If he had a flaw, it was that he was a bit high-strung. Younger Josh was excitable, particularly on special occasions such as Christmas, a birthday or a trip to his grandmother's house. Those were three occasions when Gramma tended to be around, so she had witnessed a few episodes when Josh would get a little out of control. Eventually he would want something he couldn't have—say, permission to open his Christmas presents before the adults were ready. When he didn't get his wish, he would throw a small tantrum.

Josh's dad, who was a strict disciplinarian from a military background, would not put up with what he called "Josh's meltdowns." He would call out sharply, "Joshua!" When the boy was younger, of course, that wouldn't be enough to quiet him. He would cry, roll on the floor, kick. But he soon found out that Dad wouldn't permit any further foolishness. Punishment would *not* be light. As the boy grew, he learned what the limits were, and he fearfully stayed within them.

By the time he was eight, Josh was the type of boy that adults applauded for his deportment. He never seemed to step out of line. His grades at school were exemplary. He played youth football and baseball, excelling at both. From time to time, Josh would test the boundaries, as any child will. If he was told that he could not go outside to play, he might begin to protest. But all he needed was one piercing glance of the right kind from his parents, one sharp "Josh!"—and that was that. He would become quiet and sullen, yet always do what was expected to avoid the strict punishment that inevitably followed disobedience.

Gramma had seen the extreme effectiveness of strict discipline with Josh. She had to admit that he was an attractive, well-behaved boy, with high potential. But something about the commandingly severe approach worried her, particularly when she watched the younger Josh closely. There was something strange, something a little frightening in his eyes as he submitted once again to the cut-and-dried law of "Because I said so." Gramma could only remind herself that Josh's dad seemed to know what he was doing; Josh was an outstanding young man who never got into trouble.

That is, until these past few months.

At the beginning of his ninth-grade year, things had suddenly changed. Poor grades began to come home. Nearly every Sunday morning, when it was time to go to church, he protested that he was sick—an odd development, because his best friends had been in the youth group. Then there was a series of fights that began in his physical education class and spilled into other parts of his high school existence. Some of the school officials actually claimed that Josh was the one picking the fights. *Surely that had to be a mistake,* Gramma thought. *Josh was a quiet boy, an obedient young man. He had never been in a fight in his life until very recently.*

And now, by his own confession, he was a thief. Josh made no attempt to cover for himself, admitting without a qualm that he took money from an open locker. He only seemed to regret getting caught.

His grandmother simply couldn't process the information. How could a human being completely change personality overnight? What in the world was going on with her beloved grandchild?

## THE ANGER GENERATION

Anger has permeated our culture. I'm not talking about obvious symptoms. The really dangerous stuff is often so subtle and quiet that you don't readily notice it. But walk through any business office and listen to the discussions between coworkers and you'll find that people are very resentful, not only toward their supervisors but also toward nearly anyone else in their life. They're mad at their spouses, so that more marriages than ever before are on the rocks. They're angry at political candidates, their neighbors, their pastors, the coaches of their Little League teams, even their own children.

Climb into your car and take a drive down a busy highway at rush hour. What do you notice? Anger. It even has a name—road rage. Notice how disproportionate road rage seems to be based on the situations that inspire it. Wait just an extra second before moving forward when the light turns green and someone behind you will sit on his horn. Ever notice the glaring faces of people behind the wheel? Walk through the mall or the shopping center. Listen to how people deal with sales personnel or with servers at a restaurant. We're living in an era of rudeness; but what is causing the rudeness? It's merely a symptom of anger.

For the past few years, I have worked with a movement in support of ministers who have been emotionally abused by their church congregations. These are people of God we're talking about, and yet even in the church world, we find overflowing anger. Countless pastors are leaving the ministry as a vocation because they have been treated with incredible cruelty by parishioners. If the church can't model loving behavior, what hope is there for the rest of the world?

I personally believe that anger is the driving force in this contemporary culture. It's a toxic substance, something that consumes people inwardly and then outwardly. Anger is a part of life, now as always, but it can and must be managed. Why do so few people have the expertise to handle their anger? Many of our parents couldn't handle their own anger, so how could they possibly teach their children to do so? Some of these adults dealt with anger by letting it all hang out; others by keeping it all stuffed in. Both of these techniques are misguided and dangerous in their own ways, and children learn them when offered no other model.

I have no information about how you have managed anger throughout your life or taught your children to manage anger. Maybe anger has been a problem in your family, and maybe not at all. But it's important to look at both generations that followed yours in your family. What have you observed about their methods of handling anger? As an "elder statesman" in your family, you have an opportunity to help your children and their children work with this one factor that will determine so much of their future happiness.

If your grandchild can learn to successfully navigate the turbulent emotions he finds within himself, he will be so much more successful in life. If he can't, he may be his own worst enemy in achieving the goals that he, his parents and you want him to reach. Anger management is simply that critical.

As we talk about anger, keep in mind that it's not a sin. Notice how the Bible deals with it: " 'In your anger do not sin': Do not let the sun go down while you are still angry, and do not give the devil a foothold" (Eph. 4:26-27). Anger is not sin in itself, but it can be a nesting place for sin to grow and take wing. There are times to be angry in life, and we should all be angry about the right things. The great question is what we do with our anger and, particularly, *when* we need to do something about it. Suppressed anger grows like a cancer until it is out of proportion to whatever inspired it.

I've seen anger destroy many families and individuals. Even if you don't perceive it to be a problem among the people you love, take special note of this chapter. I believe the concepts here can be lifesavers.

## Rapid Response

Why is anger in the air all around us? Is the world that much worse? Partially, yes. As we've seen in the first chapter, our culture has been negatively disrupted by a number of forces. In addition, we haven't done a good job teaching our children what to do. People come by their anger naturally but have no understanding of how to handle it. They end up doing something destructive with their emotions and making *other* people angry. The wildfire continues to spread, and the world grows angrier.

What mistakes have you made in life because of uncontrolled negative feelings? What regrets have you lived with? If it's happened to you, you can remember saying, "Why did I do that? What got control of me? How could I say and do what I did?" And you've learned that once a bell is rung, it cannot be un-rung; sometimes the damage takes a long time to repair.

But what if things were different? What if we understood exactly what anger was, how it works within us and what we should do about it?

In the simplest terms, it could be said that we have three alternative reactions to anger: word, action and avoidance (suppression). A young child lacks the verbal skills to deal with anger in words, and also the self-control required for suppression. Therefore, the child will deal with anger through action in very immature and unpleasant behavior: tears and tantrums, for example. As the child learns to use words, he may add an immature version of word use: whining. An annoyed parent will try to stifle all of these behaviors. Like Josh's dad, he may raise his voice and simply forbid any expression of the anger. If the parent shouts at the child, that parent is also expressing anger, which only reinforces and increases the anger of the child.

We don't want the noise, the emotional mess and the unpleasantness of anger. Meanwhile, the child is struggling to control negative emotions—no wonder, since we as adults have that same struggle. There are two equal and opposite mistakes that parents make in dealing with the anger of a child. First, they might ignore it and let the child ventilate the anger. Many parents today simply give up and impose no discipline or restraints at all. Despite the misconceptions people often have about venting, it's not a healthy way to handle anger. Studies show that venting does not disperse negative emotions, but actually reinforces them.

Second, we might try to stifle a child's anger, as Josh's father did. Suppressed anger does not go away, though its symptoms may be invisible for the time being. Suppressed anger will reappear, and when it does, it will repay its suppression with interest, doing much more damage than if it had been effectively handled earlier.

Anger, then, must be dealt with in a timely fashion. And these words are in no way offered to minimize the difficulty of dealing with that anger. Parents are wearier than ever from the stress of their lives; they're not always at their best when they are with their children. Grandparents often have even less energy or patience. It's difficult to handle children and the challenges that come with them. There is a great deal of pressure that you and the parents face in handling turbulent emotions—your own as well.

But we don't have the option to ignore this problem and pretend it will care for itself. Our children need our help too urgently. When you are with your grandchild and you're facing an eruption of anger, you have a golden opportunity to point the way to the mature handling of anger and make a difference that will resonate throughout the life of your family.

At the same time, you will find that your own anger is dispersed more cleanly and that you experience greater peace of mind as a result.

The two greatest dangers about anger in the child's home are these:

1. *Disruption of the love between parent and child.* At all times in the growth and life of the child, he must feel a consistent flow of unconditional love and acceptance from his parents. The presence of anger (on either side) can become a powerful obstacle.

2. *Parents dumping their anger on the child.* Mothers and fathers have no idea how much damage they can do by allowing their child to become the receptacle of their own anger. They bring home negative emotions from the workplace,

from tensions within the marriage or from someplace else. They may become frustrated at the child's immaturity, reacting in a way the child will experience as unloving.

In both cases, grandparents can virtually save the day. They can provide consistent love even when there are tensions between parent and child. And they can provide a buffer for some of the anger that could be dumped on the children. Mothers in particular receive so much anger at home. Their own parents—the children's grandparents—can gently help them express and vacate some of these volatile emotions.

Although that may be unpleasant for you—we would all like to experience the best and most pleasant behavior our loved ones can offer—you, as a mature human being, can handle someone else's anger better than a child can. Are you willing to help your adult child defuse his or her anger? Can you become a buffer so that your grandchild receives his parents' love without disruption?

## What Lies Within Us

We need to understand just how complex God has made us. We have a physical component—the body; but we also have nonphysical components—the mind, emotions and spirit. This much we all realize. Yet even when we consider the mental and emotional components of a person, there are layers within layers.

For example, at any given moment you have conscious thoughts. At this moment, your conscious thoughts are, hopefully, on the words you're reading in this sentence and the train of thought I've been carrying through these last two paragraphs. Perhaps if you could make a transcription of your conscious thoughts through the day, something like the transcript of a legal proceeding, you would recognize each thought, because you were conscious of each one.

But all the while there is another transcript going on without your true awareness of it. This is the flow of your *subconscious* thoughts. Let's look at an example of how all this works. Think about one of your adult children. If thoughts of that child come to your mind during the day, what would those thoughts concern? You might consciously wonder where she was, what she was doing, whether she has decided on her Christmas plans, or something along those lines. Meanwhile, your unconscious thoughts would be more emotional in nature: your feelings of love for that child; your feelings of fear for the child's future; your feelings of regret about past disagreements. There is a whole cluster of unconscious associations in us when we think about a family member, a traditional holiday, our hometown, one political party, the other political party, the concept of America, our faith feelings, or anything else.

Conscious feelings come from our rational decisions and intentions: *I wonder where my daughter is today? I wonder if I should call her and ask about Christmas?*

Unconscious feelings come from the experiences of life and the emotional impact those experiences have had on us: *My daughter is precious to me . . . I worry that her life is too hectic, and it will damage her marriage . . . I wonder if she is still angry with me about that incident when she was a teenager?*

Now consider that your conscious thoughts and decisions are shaped by your unconscious thoughts and feelings. As a matter of fact, far more of a person's daily life is based on unconscious factors than we realize. Most of us believe ourselves to be very rational and objective people who make careful, well-considered decisions. But why is it that you refuse to eat certain foods, knowing that most people enjoy that food? Why do you insist on wearing a certain color of shirt on this particular day? What causes you to constantly listen for words of approval from your spouse or your friend?

Life is not neat. As we move through it, we are left with impressions, hurts, joys and powerful experiences that mark us and influence all that we do afterward. Bill hates clowns because of a circus experience in his childhood. Betty won't visit a Baptist church because of something that happened in a church 30 years ago, five states away. Erma orders clam chowder everywhere she goes, thinking it will taste the way it did on a wonderful day in the city years ago, when she was a child. She doesn't actually remember that occasion, but she continues to order clam chowder.

In many instances we're unaware of the unconscious reasons that we make this move or that one. We live the illusion of being perfectly rational in every decision. All the while, in so many ways, we are at least partially the products of our experiences and how they affected us. We have emotionally unfinished business with regard to our parents, siblings, social standing, self-worth, sexuality and our feelings about religion.

Now what does all this have to do with being a grandparent? It has a great deal to do with the forces of anger that are in your grandchild, in your adult child and even in you. You need to understand that there are many hidden motives and feelings that affect the way your grandchild behaves.

## PUNISHMENT, PAIN AND PARENTING

Keeping in mind these unconscious feelings, let's turn to the important matter of punishment. Let me first make an important distinction. What is the difference between discipline and punishment? Punishment is penalizing someone as a form of negative reinforcement. Discipline refers to the area of training and guidance toward a desired goal. We'll have an entire chapter on discipline, which is a wonderful ongoing process with our children. Punishment, on the other hand, is but one category of discipline, and in fact, it's the final and least desirable option.

Over the years, I've discovered that many parents fail to miss that important distinction. They believe that punishment is the key to good training for children. In reality, punishment can be very dangerous.

When a child demonstrates anger, perhaps by yelling or slamming a door, a parent (possibly spurred by her own anger) imposes swift and severe punishment. *This will teach him a lesson,* the parent thinks. And it does. But over time it can teach other things too.

Researchers "teach" laboratory rats to behave in some ways and not behave in others by applying mild electrical shocks or by withholding food pellets. It works; in time, the rat will do exactly what the researcher desires. Why are human beings any different?

They're different because they have human emotions. We can change behavior, but we may also damage emotions if we apply punishment unwisely. Let's consider the situation with Josh. His father applied the equivalent of the electric shock whenever Josh showed inappropriate expressions of anger as a child. In time, Josh learned to behave exactly the way his parents wanted him to behave. But his actions were not motivated by emotional maturity. They were driven by fear and dread, and a residue of frustration and anger began to build.

Josh's case is like so many I've observed. Bewildered parents have brought me children who were so obedient, so appealing and so successful in school and social life. Then something changed. That obedient, successful daughter suddenly became pregnant or involved with precisely the type of young man that would most shock her parents. A son might go from Eagle Scout and church youth leader to drug dealer. It always seemed inexplicable, but a few questions would tell the story. There was deep anger in the child. The anger had no outlet, so it festered inside. The anger could never be expressed in normal situations and eventually came out in some irrational and surprising way.

On each occasion when Josh behaved or felt angry, if the situation had been handled more wisely than it was, there would have been no unresolved anger to be pushed inside the child where it built toward something more dangerous. In other words, Josh was not taught to behave maturely and appropriately; he was simply taught how to avoid punishment. His unresolved feelings joined that complex network of unconscious thoughts and emotions that lie beneath the surface. Like toxic waste, they polluted everything else down there.

It's also important to understand that the anger is not ultimately expressed in proportion to its earlier cause. For Josh, it was a history of "little" things: No, he couldn't play outside after dinner; no, he couldn't have a second helping of ice cream; no, he couldn't have Freddy over to spend the night. Note also that, in themselves, these were all reasonable stances for the parents to take. The problem was that Josh was angry and had no help in resolving his anger. When the anger eventually came out, it emerged through behavior far more serious than second helpings of ice cream. Josh wasn't aware that he stole the money or provoked fights as a way of striking back at his parents. His decisions were unconscious.

The name I have given this phenomenon is "stealth anger." The more common term, you may already know, is *passive-aggressive* anger. There are so many misunderstandings about that term that I've chosen to use my own. I call it stealth anger because it lurks silently within and moves undetected toward its deadly destination like a stealth jet or missile.

What about your own emotions? Have you ever lost your temper while dealing with a child? As a parent and grandparent, you know how easy that is. Just remember: *The most certain way to invoke stealth anger in children is to dump our own anger upon them*, for nothing causes deeper resentment and frustration than becoming the brunt of a more powerful person's negative emotions. The message the child receives is this: "You may not express your anger—but I can." This is all the more confusing to the child, and all the more reason to be angry.

## Managing Your Anger

If you're a grandparent who is doing a good bit of the parenting, your patience will be tried. Let me give you a few practical tips to help you manage your own anger.

1. *Keep a journal.* Record your thoughts and frustrations at the end of each day. Seek to get an objective picture of your emotions. Review what you've written daily and set new strategies for handling the challenges before you. You'll receive a lot of strength from this discipline.

2. *Discuss your feelings with an adult*—your adult child, the other parent or your spouse, as applicable. This will be a helpful way to deal with your own emotions without venting them upon your grandchild.

3. *Seek assistance* from friends to help you care for the children.

4. *Pray.* It sounds trite, but it's a powerful resource. Ask God to give you strength and self-control in managing your emotions so you can be a good role model for your grandchild.

## RECOGNIZING THE REAL ISSUE

What about children and their anger? Before offering some examples of the right responses to a child's anger, I want to issue a warning about one particular wrong response. I've seen this mistake become more prevalent in recent months. I'd thought that our unfortunate cultural phase of heavy-handed authoritarian punishment was over. We've seen so much anger in the recent generation who have been over-spanked and over-punished, and I assumed that counselors were beginning to learn the terrible mistake in punishment-based discipline.

But actually, I'm hearing more instruction along the lines of "the need for stronger discipline." If the child seems to have a strong will and doesn't immediately obey, parents are directed to aggressively punish and break the will. There are times when that can be the worst thing you can do. The classic example is the child between the ages of two and three. We all know the favorite word of that stage of childhood: "No!"

You ask the child to clean up his toys and he barks out "No!" You ask him if he'd like a hot dog for lunch, and he says, "No!"

When we understand what is really happening here, we don't grit our teeth and start setting penalties; we laugh! This is actually a well-known cycle of *individuation* in which the child is establishing his own identity. There will be other times in the child's life when that becomes important, adolescence being the other crucial cycle of becoming separate. But I want parents and grandparents to understand that this is not about disobedience. Your child actually wants and intends to obey, if you can simply be patient and understand what is happening. Reacting in a heavy-handed way every time a child says the word "no" can cause terrible damage to that young life. Why? Heavy-handed discipline hampers a child's exploration of his own identity as distinct from the will of his parents. There is nothing unhealthy about that—on the contrary, it's central and crucial in human development.

My son once called me on the phone in a fit of laughter. He said, "Dad, listen to this." He then proceeded to ask his two-year-old child if he wanted to do one thing, another thing, or still another. Every time, my grandson said, "No!" I had taught my adult son about human development, so he understood that this was a time to be patient. We had a good laugh about it. There will be other times, of course, when his son tests the true boundaries of discipline and obedience. Those will be times for training and character shaping.

There are times for children and also for teenagers when young people are simply figuring out who they are as individual human beings. Therefore, let's take a look at some right responses to a child's anger.

## RIGHT RESPONSES

*First, fill the emotional tank.* We've talked about creating the right emotional atmosphere. Do all you can to fill your grandchild's emotional tank. However, that must also be done at the child's home. You don't have the power as a grandparent to control what goes on in the home environment, but give your grandchild unconditional love in all the ways we discussed earlier. If you can, talk to the child's parents about providing love in the right way. So many of the problems we dread will never materialize when a child simply knows that he is loved and accepted. When anger does cause problems, the well-loved child will always be easier to handle. Your grandchild will be dealing from a foundation of strength rather than emotional insecurity.

*Second, recognize anger for what it is.* Stealth anger is deceptive. It seems disconnected to any causality or rational reasoning. If you were to tell Josh's dad that his son is acting out his anger toward his parents, Josh's dad would likely reply, "Mad at us? But what have we done? Things were very peaceful before this rash of unacceptable events." It's important to understand the nature of stealth anger and recognize the underlying causes. The child may be angry for many different reasons, though the home situation is always the most likely, because a loving home is the child's greatest need.

*Third, talk about it.* Your opportunity as a grandparent is to have a meaningful conversation with your grandchild at those very times when he may be uncommunicative with his parents. This has certainly been my experience. It won't happen automatically, of course, but only as you develop that trusting and affectionate relationship. Your grandchild needs to know that you will listen nonjudgmentally. He needs to know that he can open up when he is with you, and that you're not simply a representative of his parents. If you want to build that level of trust, be patient and loving as you wait for your grandchild to find the moment when he'll discuss his feelings. Remember also that there's a very good chance that he doesn't even realize why he's angry. He will have to sort through many thoughts and emotions; a patient and loving grandparent can be the one to help him do it.

Again, anger can be expressed in three ways: through *words*, through *behavior*, and through *inaction, or suppression*. Only the first way is healthy. By the time you even have this discussion, the other two have probably already been tried, with the damage done. Now it's time to do things the right way and learn to verbalize the negative emotions. Anger can be discharged without harm through the right use of words. And how is that accomplished?

There is an ascending scale that represents what we want to happen as we deal with anger verbally. It begins at the most accessible level and becomes more difficult, requiring more maturity, as we move to each new level. Reach the final level and you have mastered your anger. Here is the scale.

## Handling Anger

**4** | **Internally**—Finding ways to resolve it within yourself

**3** | **Interpersonally**—Resolving it with the person with whom you're angry

**2** | **Pleasantly**—Discussing in a calm and conversational tone

**1** | **Verbally**—Whining, complaining or venting

## Verbally

A child initially handles anger in the form of whining, complaining or venting. Nobody likes to be exposed to any of that, yet even this lowest level of anger management is preferable to stuffing the anger or acting it out. Let's imagine that you have a grandson like Josh, who is a teenager. If your grandson speaks at all about what is bothering him, that's better than silence. It may not be enjoyable to hear, and you may want to tell him, "No, you're looking at this thing all wrong!" But verbalization, no matter how immature, is a beginning. It's no fun to listen to what is unpleasant, but it's far better than diverting the anger toward a more serious expression later on.

## Pleasantly

The next goal is to train a child to express his anger not only verbally, but pleasantly. This takes a bit more self-control and maturity. It is the difference between "Everybody hates me" and "Sometimes it feels to me as if no one cares about me." It is also different in that the tone is not whiny or temperamental; it is calm and conversational. With a small child who is whining, we don't say, "Be quiet and go to your room." We say, "Let's see if we can discuss this in a more pleasant way." With a teenager, we might simply listen to the negative and immature expression for a moment. If we are attentive, supportive and active in filling the emotional tank, the teenager's emotions will eventually calm down. He will find that he can discuss his feelings much more rationally and pleasantly.

## Interpersonal Resolution

Quite frankly, most people today never reach phase two—expressing anger verbally and pleasantly. However, when we've attained the ability to express our anger verbally and pleasantly, the next goal is something even more difficult: resolving anger with the one at whom it is directed. What a wonderful moment when any of us can sit down with someone and resolve a conflict as two mature and emotionally healthy individuals. The New Testament, from the Gospels to the letters of Paul, is filled with this mark of genuine spirituality. Yet even when we have the maturity to do that, the other person may not. Therefore, we must always have the option that is the fourth phase.

## Internal Resolution

This must be accomplished even when another person isn't involved. Sometimes we're not angry at another person. Sometimes we're angry at life itself. We could be angry with an entire school or church. Then, of course, it's entirely possible that sitting down with another person isn't an option. Going back to our example of Josh, it could be that

Josh's Gramma works with him over a period of time and helps him realize his anger and resolve to master it. It would be unfortunate if Josh's father were incapable of having such a discussion, but sometimes that's the case. A grandparent may have to make the call. The point is that the ultimate goal for any person is to learn to manage anger on the inside so that it doesn't remain there.

## How Stealth Anger Works

There is a reason that the Bible tells us not to let the sun set upon our anger (see Eph. 4:26). Never abide by the myth about "shaking it off and feeling better about it tomorrow." A very small frustration can be handled that way. But when we're really angry, we must deal with our feelings promptly. Why? Because stealth anger is the most dangerous force within us. Let's take a closer look at how it works.

Anger wants free rein. It seeks a way out, whether healthy (now) or unhealthy (later). It will be expressed verbally (now) or behaviorally (later). The immediate verbal expression will probably be unpleasant. But when those emotions are redirected, pushed deep inside, we harbor something unhealthy. It lurks in the complex of unconscious thoughts and feelings within until it finds a stealthy escape in the form of some indirect act of anger.

Stealth anger is manipulative. In one way or another, it will strike out at someone or something, sooner or later. The victims of a person's stealth anger often have no relationship to what originally caused the anger. A contemporary example is the terrible plight of many ministers in today's church. They become lightning rods for every manner of anger that can be found among the people in their congregation. Have they done anything to deserve so much mistreatment? Usually not. People will dump their anger over everything else that has happened in their lives—anger that no one taught them to manage properly.

There are two components of stealth anger. The first is an anti-authority approach to life that is usually fairly conscious and intentional. People under the influence of stealth anger will resist virtually every form of authority, whether it is a traffic light, a committee chairman, a pastor or a dress code on the job. The second component is less active and more passive-aggressive, usually something the person doesn't even realize. Passive-aggressive behavior sets out to hurt an authority figure but wounds the angry person instead. The most common example is the student who makes bad grades because it's a sure way to hurt the parents. The primary victim, however, is the student himself.

I should also mention that a certain amount of passive-aggressive behavior is actually normal, just a part of early adolescent development. I once visited my child's school on Parent Night and looked into the kids' desks, where there were many assignments that hadn't been turned in. The teacher confirmed my suspicions: The class had an epidemic of late completion for its work. I knew that kids around 13 or 14 tend to have a passive-aggressive streak, and they will refuse to turn in their papers even though they've done the work.

Usually this milder form of stealth anger is a phase that passes. But when there is a more serious problem, stealth anger becomes the primary method of handling negative emotion, and that's when there's a danger. How does stealth anger manifest? Here are three primary traits of stealth anger:

1. *It is irrational.* You will be bewildered by the fact that your grandchild continues to take actions that make no sense at all. Why not turn in a homework assignment if you've completed it? It's not about making sense, but about expressing anger.

2. *It is unmanageable.* Since adults tend to be rational people, they will take rational steps to "fix" the situation. The struggling student will get a tutor who could be the greatest teacher in

the world, but nothing will change for the student. Parents or grandparents may offer incredible incentives: "Pass that course and I'll take you and your best friend on a skiing trip" or "I'll buy you a new stereo." That's the wrong approach anyway, of course, but it will also be ineffective. This is not about the specific behavior, but about expressing anger.

3. *It is self-inflicted.* I have touched on this sad fact already. The greatest victim of stealth anger is the child himself. Josh will start fights and lose them. He will steal from a friend, knowing that he will be caught. In every case, he seeks to hurt his father but becomes his own collateral damage. Angry young ladies will get pregnant or marry someone completely wrong for them, and they're the ones who will pay the greatest price. Young men will get addicted to drugs and ruin their lives, simply to inflict hurt on someone else. Yet they do it because it's not about their own pain, but about expressing anger.

Another sign of stealth anger is that it comes in the very area calculated to hurt the object of the anger. Josh deprived himself of his church youth group because he knew his parents cared deeply about his spiritual growth. Young people tend to act out their anger in the directions of church, school grades and choice of peer group, because these are lightning-rod issues with their parents.

We can't fix the situation by bargaining with our teenagers, by sending them away to boarding school, by putting them in a detox facility, or any other "rational" strategy other than dealing directly with the anger itself. There is going to be a certain amount of rebellious behavior during the teen years, and we simply have to manage these times and keep the anger from becoming more serious. Therefore, it's a good idea for parents and grandparents to encourage, for example, healthy and wholesome physical activities such as backpacking trips, ropes courses and skiing. These appeal to the healthy energy and adrenaline that teenagers have, and they keep the young person engaged in a positive way with the world. And wherever possible, the teenager should be allowed to express his own identity, choose his own friends and so on in ways that help him take ownership of who he is becoming.

## THE ANGER LADDER

Around the age of 17, if grandparents and parents have done a good job, a child may have acquired the maturity and ability to handle anger maturely. It doesn't happen routinely, of course—not in today's world. Many adults, regardless of age, haven't gotten there. But in the best case, my observation is that 17 is the golden year when a young person has a reasonable opportunity to reach the goal of good anger management.

But what happens on the way there? To illustrate the range of behaviors, beginning with the least mature and ascending toward the most mature, the "Anger Ladder" is a tool I've used to help others understand the behaviors of anger management.

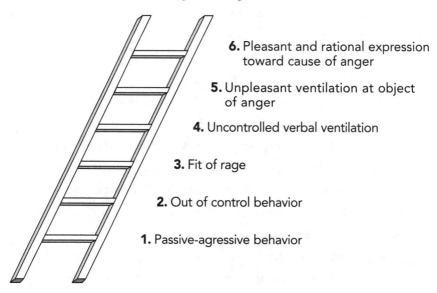

**6.** Pleasant and rational expression toward cause of anger

**5.** Unpleasant ventilation at object of anger

**4.** Uncontrolled verbal ventilation

**3.** Fit of rage

**2.** Out of control behavior

**1.** Passive-agressive behavior

Take a few moments to study the Anger Ladder. It helps to show the process of "climbing" toward acceptable and effective behavior. No one begins in the middle; all of us have to start at the bottom and painfully work our way upward. And no one really makes much progress before the age of six. At that age, we use the simple goal of teaching a child to express anger verbally. But as a child is helped and guided by loving adults, the process of emotional growth should take place.

Where is your grandchild on this ladder? What progress have you seen, and how close is he or she to the next rung? One thing is certain: the ladder can be "polished" with constant application of unconditional love. The more the child is loved, the stronger and more rapid will be his or her ascent. And if the time comes that your grandchild slips a rung or two downward, you shouldn't panic. The ages and stages of life, particularly in adolescence, can make it seem as if the child is moving in the wrong direction, when that isn't necessarily the case.

## Adult Anger

It's also important to consider the emotions that you and the parents of the child experience. Is anger an issue in your life? What about the life of your adult child and/or your adult child's spouse? Have you looked at the ladder with yourself in mind?

Earlier in this chapter, I suggested that you talk about your feelings with another adult, and perhaps keep a journal of your emotions. While you're doing so, keep an eye on the child's parents. As you already realize, no one in the world is more important to the emotional development of your grandchild. As a grandparent, you can make many vital and wonderful differences, but if the parent is struggling, there are limits to what can be done.

Be as patient as you possibly can with that parent. Listen and be affirming, just as you would with your grandchild. Adults also need to have their emotional tanks filled. Is anyone doing that for your adult child, or the spouse? Again, as we discussed in the chapter concerning helping the parents, it's a great idea to spend special time with the parent or parents, when the child is elsewhere. Go out to eat together or take a walk together. Encourage the parent to talk, and you can find an opportunity to discuss some of the anger management insights that are found in this chapter.

When the child himself is trying your patience, use self-talk as a safeguard. For example, the child may be whining, complaining or some other kind of negative behavior that has the potential of setting off your own anger. If you lose your temper, you lose a precious opportunity to set an example for the child; you also increase the anger load the child must handle. Therefore, talk to yourself. (No, it doesn't mean you're crazy—sometimes it's the way to prevent that!) You can say something like this:

> My grandchild is very definitely a child. That's the way children act. It's not pleasant, but it's something I can handle. I am not a child, and I will not act as if I am. God will give me the strength to be patient. I'm going to overcome my temptation to blow my top, and I'm going to show this child what emotional maturity and self-control are, if it's the last thing I do!

Here's an example of prayer that also serves as positive self-talk:

> Dear Lord, thank You for the opportunity of this moment, even if feels like a trial. My grandchild is bringing his anger to me instead of somewhere less positive. I have the chance to teach a lesson. Help me to make the very most of this chance!

## FIVE FINAL TIPS

*Be patient but firm.* I have stressed patience and love, because they are so important and because so many parents vent their own anger on their children. As you'll see in our chapter on discipline, I do *not* advocate letting children behave without requirements or restrictions. This is really the equal and opposite error that some parents make because they're trying to be cold authoritarians. Be loving, gentle, patient and kind. Always listen. But never change the rules. If you have set the boundaries, you must be consistent with them. Once you budge, you've opened yourself to manipulation by your grandchild.

*Be a calming influence.* Your grandchild may come to you in all the turbulence of his emotions. My granddaughter knew that there were times when she could come and simply be held quietly for a while. As she was on her way to my home, I would draw her a warm bath—a wonderful, calming influence in itself. Nothing can be accomplished while either grandparent or grandchild is distressed. Adrenaline flows, and we call this "flooding." If you, your grandchild or your grandchild's parent is particularly overwrought, take several quiet hours before you talk about the matter. Make it clear that you do want to hear everything, but there needs to be a cooling period first.

*Be accepting.* Remember what "unconditional" means. There will be no condemnation. You don't agree with or endorse all things that might have been done, but you are not going to preach sermons. If you were, your grandchild would never come to you. He needs an ear to hear and a shoulder to lean upon. At a time like this, you can prove forever the power of your love for your grandchild.

*Be redemptive.* What has your grandchild done *right*? There is always something positive to underline. In times of anger, people feel bad about themselves. They hurt for many reasons and need comfort. It helps when you say, "I know this is a rough situation, and I know how you must feel. But I want you to know that I see so much growth in you, because this time you didn't (shout, slam a door, insult someone, whatever)."

*Be resourceful.* When you've done all these things, you will have created a teachable moment. Your grandchild will have heard you, and therefore will be capable of listening. He will not have been judged, so he will be capable of judging himself. He will be calm, and therefore able to think positively and rationally. Now you have the opportunity to point toward a better way of doing things. As much as you can, point without giving all the answers. Ask questions: "What do you think would be a better way of handling things? What is the first thing you think you'll do to make things right?"

Sometimes you may think of an episode in your own life that will be helpful to relate. Your grandchild has come to you in a time of storm, an angry time. Whether he knows it or not, he craves the wisdom of your years. What a time of treasure, when you can pour out that wisdom and make a difference in a young life.

# 7

# The Discipline Your Grandchild Needs

E d, known to his grandchildren as Pops, has just poured a fresh glass of lemonade and headed for the patio. There he finds his favorite chair and settles comfortably into it. It's a beautiful spring day, and he's enjoying the sight of a father teaching his son how to throw and catch a baseball. Jamie, the father, and Drew, the son, are Ed's son and grandson, respectively.

Ed heaves a sigh of relief as he sees the pleasure of the two of them throwing, popping their gloves with their fists and catching the ball. Several minutes ago, when Jamie invited his son, Drew, for a lesson, Ed had caught himself grimacing. He didn't want there to be any unpleasantness; why, this could all end up with Jamie shouting and little Drew crying. That was Ed's first reaction.

Then he had heard the laughter. He stood at the window and watched how Jamie stooped beside his son and gently instructed him on how to "look the ball into" the glove; how to let it hit the webbing and slide into the palm; how to use the free hand to keep the ball from escaping. Ed shook his head in wonder; Jamie just might turn out to be a better dad than he had been. That was when he poured the glass of lemonade and joined the two others outdoors.

Ed's thoughts slid backward in time, back to an amazingly distant period, some five decades earlier—a time when Ed was no larger than little Drew here. On another lawn, far away from this spot, in a field that is now a shopping center, Father had tried to teach the same lesson. Ed could remember no laughter, no gentle words on that occasion.

On that steamy July day, Ed had worn a tattered black baseball glove that must have been handed down by some cousin or other relative. Father had worn no glove at all; he simply caught the ball with his good hand before hurling it back. Father was a man's man, that was for certain. He taught this lesson as he did everything else—with unsmiling determination that bordered on fury. The lesson must be learned rapidly and well, or you would see the steel in his eye and hear the anger in his voice.

"You're afraid of it! Afraid of the ball!" he snapped. "You get those 'happy feet' before it even gets there, and you shut your eyes and turn your face. You can't catch the ball when you're afraid of it!"

What could Ed say? All he could do was grit his teeth, try to be a little man, and try clamping his sneakers to the dry ground as he faced the next throw. Father always hurled the ball back at him, at a fair velocity, the second he caught it. Ed never seemed quite set to make the catch. And when, inevitably enough, the ball hit him right on the ear, he could not keep himself from crying, half in pain and half in frustration.

There was no sympathy to be had from Father, of course. He scowled as he walked over to pick up the ball. "Nothing but a baby," he said as he began walking home. "Tell me when you're ready to grow up, and we'll try again."

Ed relives it all now, for the first time in decades, surprised by how much emotion he still feels over the memory. He barely catches a tear before it escapes the corner of his eye.

Ed takes a healthy swallow of lemonade and watches how Jamie and Drew approach the same father-son ritual. It seems nearly miraculous. Jamie has bought a glove for himself and a smaller matching one for his son. He works not with a genuine horsehide baseball, but a plastic replica that wouldn't hurt if it hit Drew. His soft tosses are easy enough for a child to catch, and with each success, Daddy shouts encouragement. Ed finds himself getting into the spirit: "Great grab, Drew—you're a natural! That's my grandson!"

Little Drew's smile is as wide as the brim on his oversized cap.

"Wow, you're way ahead," says Jamie, walking over to his son. "You've got a knack for catching the ball. Let me show you something about throwing." The father slowly pulls his arm above and behind his head, demonstrating how to use the arm, rather than the wrist, to make a throw. He urges Drew to try it without the ball. "That's it," he says. "But let's see if we can keep our arm up and down, like this, instead of to the side."

Ed watches the two of them work on the right motion for throwing a baseball. Drew is making good progress. Sometimes, of course, he forgets some part of the mechanics. When that happens, his father gently pauses and shows him how to correct his motion.

When it's all over, the two of them walk back inside the house, Jamie's arm encircling his son's little shoulder. Drew can't seem to stop smiling. Neither can his grandfather.

## The True Nature of Discipline

Have you ever played word association? I say a word, and you say the first thing that comes into your mind. For example, if I say, "dog," you might say, "cat." That kind of thing.

If I say "discipline," what is the first idea that comes to mind? What word would leap off the tip of your tongue?

For many people, that word would be something like "punishment." Traditionally, when we speak of disciplining a child, we think of applying some form of punishment. To be truthful, I'm very concerned when I think about the tendency of most people to make that association. Discipline is a wonderful thing, and it takes in so much more than punishment, which is its last resort and most negative facet.

A much better synonym for "discipline" would be "training." That's exactly what it is. One of the four central needs of children is the need for wise and positive training toward emotional and spiritual maturity. We always begin with love, filling the emotional tank so that the child is secure. Having built a foundation of love in the home, we have the right conditions for training the child.

But as we all know, teaching and training can be very difficult. We have to isolate the wrong habits and tendencies, then convince someone to replace them with the right ones. Let's take a classic example. A small child doesn't always want to eat the right foods. Particularly at a certain age, the child may turn up her nose at a helping of green beans or squash. So we'll make you the young parent in this example, imagining that you're facing this obstacle with your five-year-old daughter. You realize that now is the time to teach her how to enjoy eating the right foods. You have a friend who still doesn't eat right, even as an adult. Your friend's parents simply gave up, not wanting to fight this battle every single evening at the dinner table. "Eat what you want," your friend's mother finally said. "You just won't get any dessert."

After a while, of course, she forgot that part of the arrangement. There was a freshly baked cake, and Mom couldn't imagine serving everyone except her child a piece. So your friend enjoyed a nice dessert without eating her sweet potatoes.

Now, gritting your teeth and resolving not to let that happen in your house, you look at your stubborn daughter and her serving of green beans. "No!" she shouts. "I don't like 'em! I won't eat 'em!" You strongly consider taking the fork, spearing a few beans, and forcing the whole thing past those pouty lips.

Instead you sit back and think, What exactly is discipline? Is it punishing a child who won't abide by the rules, until she does abide by them? Or is it just what we've said: taking her hand and guiding her toward mature judgments and right thinking?

Punishment-based discipline is built around imposing a parent's or guardian's will on the child. Its chief tool is the power that an adult has over that child, and the rules are simple: Do as I tell you to do or you will pay the consequences. This punishment basis is highly effective at modifying behavior but, as we have seen in the previous chapter, there are unforeseen consequences. When power and punishment are at the root of a relationship, fear and resentment are the products. Anger builds, and eventually escapes through some negative form of behavior.

What is the alternative? It is what I call *need-based discipline*. Punishment-based discipline asks the question, "What do I need to do to force the right result?" But need-based parenting asks the question, "What does this child really need, and how can I help her learn how to fill that need?"

Let me assure you that I'm not advocating a loose hands-off style of parenting, in the manner of the friend's mother who gave up at the dinner table. Need-based discipline is always firm, always loving and fair. It takes a great deal more self-discipline, restraint and insight to recognize the child's need and help him or her meet it.

Think of it this way: Have you ever worked for a cold and strict boss, who simply gave orders and demanded compliance? Have you ever worked for one who was much more positive and teamwork-oriented, working beside you to help you meet your goal? Which situation was the most productive? Which created the most frustration and ill will on your part? The opening story in this chapter offered two models of teaching. The grandfather was taught in a painful way that created fear and sadness in his heart; his own son has discovered how to make teaching fun and relationship enhancing.

Just as we would rather work under authority that is loving and fair, so do children. The real difference is the atmosphere of unconditional love that has already been set in the home. Your message is, "I love you no matter what. I love you so much that I want to help you be the best, most mature and healthy person you can be."

Does that mean, for example, that your grandchild will immediately eat the helping of green beans? No. It does mean that your grandchild is more willing to cooperate in the long run, because she feels loved and will not feel caught up in a power struggle. For the moment, there is still a certain amount of frustration for the parent or grandparent—there are no easy formulas for getting children to be perfect in every way. Need-based discipline, however, ultimately wins the race. It avoids anger and resentment, instead creating a team of parent and child working together for a mutual goal. And the older the child grows, the more she will appreciate the loving discipline she has received.

It's easy for an adult to approach discipline out of simple frustration. The misbehavior of a child is upsetting to us. We're tired at times, and we can't understand why these kids don't "get it" and do things as miniature adults would do them. When the child becomes stubborn, we become stubborn too—it's simple human nature. If we're not careful, we could get caught up in the battle of wills: "If that's the way you want to play it, grandchild, I can be just as tough." At that point, we're not thinking of the need of the child, but on winning the battle. When that happens, there are no winners. We want to be proactive as parents or grandparents, working from a foundation of love; we don't want to be reactive, simply responding negatively to negative behavior.

We can afford to take to heart these words from Paul:

But do not use your freedom to indulge the sinful nature; rather, serve one another in love. The entire law is summed up in a single command: "Love your neighbor as yourself." If you keep on biting and devouring each other, watch out or you will be destroyed by each other (Gal. 5:13-15).

As a grandparent, study the relationship between your adult child and your grandchild. Is there a truly loving spirit between them? If that unconditional love is replaced by a cold war, tragic things can happen. Parents have come to me in tears, saying something like this: "I haven't seen my daughter in five years. She wants nothing to do with me. How could that be?"

These parents loved their children, but how terribly sad that they failed to furnish love in a way that would nurture their children. Discipline in the home failed because self-discipline was not applied. In the sixth chapter of Ephesians, Paul instructs children to obey their parents. Moms and dads, naturally enough, love to quote that verse to their children. They should also note the verse that follows: "Fathers, do not exasperate your children; instead, bring them up in the training and instruction of the Lord" (Eph. 6:4).

That teaching is so important. Thirty years ago, we saw a wave of behavioral modification-based parenting models. These authoritarian principles urged parents to be completely intolerant of any disobedient behavior. As a result, many mothers and fathers adopted a harsh, punishment-driven manner that truly exasperated their children. Time and again I saw examples of young people whose behavior was exemplary for years until it suddenly erupted in waves of irrational, damaging stealth anger. To force children to behave is not the same thing as shaping their character. Only through unconditional love can we offer "the training and instruction of the Lord," in Paul's words.

## THE ROOT OF MISBEHAVIOR

We could summarize our points about discipline this way:

- Apply discipline based on a child's need rather than your frustration.
- Use self-discipline to keep your anger from overwhelming the process.

- Make sure there's an atmosphere of love rather than a battle of wills.

This is all fine and good—and surely easier said than done, even for those grandparents who don't live with their grandchildren all the time. But what about the specifics? Can we be more practical about how to apply loving discipline?

Let's look at an example concerning Ed, the grandfather from the beginning of this chapter. Later that evening, Ed sat in the living room and carried on a conversation with his son, Jamie. It's a rather serious discussion, given that Jamie is considering a change in careers. He is discussing his options with Ed.

Meanwhile, hovering just outside the conversation is Drew, the young boy. He is particularly watching Ed ("Pops"). To him, Pops is a jolly and affectionate figure. He has not often seen his grandfather acting so "grown-up." He wonders if this is still the same Pops who always teases him, plays with him, lifts him from the floor and affectionately places him in his lap. He moves over beside Ed's chair, lowers himself to the floor and slowly raises upward to peek over the arm of the chair.

Nothing happens. The grandfather is still absorbed in conversation. Drew continues to watch, a bit puzzled. Finally he taps his forefinger three times on Pops' shoulder. Pops briefly looks his way, smiles absently and turns back toward Drew's daddy. The two adults continue to converse.

Drew says, "Pops, guess what?"

Daddy says, "Drew, run along, fella. Can you go play outside so your Pops and I can talk about some important things?"

Drew walks toward the next room, heaving an exaggerated sigh for effect. Nothing works, however. He might as well be invisible.

Five minutes pass. Suddenly Ed and Jamie break off their conference as they hear Jamie's wife shout, "Drew! What do you think you're doing?"

It turns out that Drew is tossing the plastic baseball—the same one he and his daddy threw and caught—against the kitchen wall. Just as his mother caught him, a stray throw hit one of Grandmother's framed samplers and sent it crashing to the floor.

Now he has everyone's full attention. Daddy says, "What got into you, Drew? We've told you about throwing a ball indoors—particularly when you are a guest in someone's home! Well, you're going to be punished now. You must go sit outside in the car until we're ready to go home. No toys or books. Sit there and think about how you have acted."

Ed whispers, "Jamie, can I speak to you a second in the next room?"

Back in the living room, Ed says, "I think I understand what happened. Drew doesn't get to see his Pops very often. He wanted to play and he didn't have any conception of what we were talking about or how important it might be."

"That doesn't mean he has to go in the next room and throw a ball at his grandmother's picture."

"No, of course not. I just think he didn't know what else to do. He tried to get my attention and I didn't even speak to him. Would you let me spend a few minutes with him?"

"Well, of course," says Jamie, not quite understanding. "If you think that's right."

It *is* right. And no, the point is not to avoid punishing. Rather the point is that the situation arose simply because Drew needed his emotional tank to be filled, and on this occasion, he particularly needed it to be filled by his grandfather. Was it appropriate for him to interrupt the conversation? No. Was it understandable? Yes, when we make the attempt to see the situation through a young boy's eyes.

This is another example of proactive rather than reactive parenting. A proactive grandfather might realize that, even in the midst of the conversation, the little boy needed to be loved. Perhaps Pops could put him on his lap, give him a squeeze and tell him that he needed just a few minutes more for a very important conversation with Daddy. After that, they could do whatever Drew wanted. His increasing bids for attention were just his way of asking, "Do you still love me, Pops?" An adult, of course, could ask it in words; children are verbally immature and must communicate that emotion through their behavior.

A moment in the lap, a bit of eye contact and a warm word would probably be all that Drew needed. He didn't require a significant amount of attention or a special activity, just a reassurance that his beloved Pops still loved him. After that he would run along and play happily, and certainly he wouldn't have sought attention by throwing the ball indoors. Reactive parenting is waiting for the misbehavior and responding in frustration and disappointment.

## THROUGH THE EYES OF A CHILD

All misbehavior, of course, doesn't follow as a direct result of an empty emotional tank. If you love a child perfectly, there will still be some teaching and discipline to apply. But a great deal of misbehavior can certainly be avoided through the right amount of love—and then, on those less frequent occasions when there does need to be discipline, the child will be more cooperative.

You can see, then, how we tend to reverse the equation simply because we only look at things through an adult point of view. Understanding the world through a child's eyes makes a great deal of difference in working with them and loving them. For Jamie, the father, Drew's job is to "act like a big boy" by making himself scarce when the need arises. If that doesn't happen, Drew is misbehaving. Yet Drew's perspective is lacking the nuances of when he should and shouldn't be the focus of attention. His one concern is to know that he is loved. As long as his emotional tank is filled, he will be appropriately well behaved and cooperative. If the tank seems empty, he will take increasingly desperate measures to get the attention that will fill it.

In addition to his admonition for fathers not to exasperate their children (see Eph. 6:4), Paul writes, "Fathers, do not embitter your children, or they will become discouraged" (Col. 3:21). While Paul addresses fathers, his advice fits grandparents and mothers (and any other adult guardian) just as well. Remember, the apostle did not write these words last week. He wrote them 2,000 years ago, during a time when children were very often ill-treated. Yet through the love and wisdom of God, he instructs us to treat little ones with respect and dignity.

All Christian love, really, is proactive rather than reactive. It spreads love by planting it. We know that God loves us unconditionally; and only because that is true do we have the opportunity to offer the same kind of love to others. Then, as we do so, they learn how to love in the same way. "We love because he first loved us" (1 John 4:19). Please be assured that the love you give your grandchild is never a dead-end street. It will resound in his or her young life. It will be renewed in the warmth and compassion your grandchild has for others, simply because you showed him or her how to love.

Can you provide that kind of love, even when the child's behavior is unattractive and unpleasant? Can you look at the behavior and understand that it relates to a need that hasn't been met? Identifying the need, of course, is the key to guiding our grandchildren. How do we do that? In the next section, we'll explore that question.

## PHYSICAL ISSUES

The wise parent or grandparent's first question when faced with a grandchild's misbehavior is this: *Does the child need her emotional tank filled?*

In so many cases, that's the one question you need to ask. But sometimes misbehavior has other root causes. If you're quite satisfied that the emotional tank is not the problem, your next question is this one: *Is this a physical problem?*

You see, physical issues make up the second leading cause of misbehavior. You should ask, "Is my grandchild in pain? Is she ill? Is she tired, hungry, thirsty?"

Tiredness in particular will be the simple problem in a great number of cases. Many children today don't get the rest they need. They're over-stimulated by television, video games or other distractions too late in the evening. In some cases, parents are eating dinner much later due to work schedules. (Again, we see an example of an anti-child and anti-family culture that no longer allows for the needs of the nuclear family.) Bedtime for children seems to be much later than a generation ago.

Think also about the diets that children eat today. Does your grandchild get sufficient nutrition? Are there too many stimulants such as sugar or caffeine in the foods children are eating? Of course, grandparents love giving children sugary treats.

If your grandchild is visiting your home (or even when you're making the visit), it could also be that the child is stimulated by the change in the usual environment. We've all observed how children can become excited and energetic when a new "playmate" is available.

All these reasons could account for some level of misbehavior in your grandchild. Consider also the special needs that children have today. Refer to our chapter devoted to that subject.

Whatever physical issue might possibly be at the root of the behavior, once you identify it, the solution should be obvious.

## Five Keys for Correction

Sometimes misbehavior is simply misbehavior. It could be that the child is testing the boundaries. *Mommy and Daddy don't allow this particular behavior, so let's see if Grandmother does.* In such a case, the emotional tank would not be the issue; neither would there be any particular physical origin to the problem. How do you handle normal misbehavior in your grandchild?

The first rule is never to lose control of your household. If a child believes she can take control by manipulating adults in any way, she'll make that attempt every time. You must be very firm while remaining loving. I've isolated five potential responses for an adult. I want you to take special notice of whether they are positive or negative, for obviously we want to discipline in a positive way whenever possible. Sometimes, however, we may have to choose a negative response. A third option is neutral and is reserved for special situations. Here are the five and their positive-negative orientation:

| | |
|---|---|
| Requests | Positive |
| Commands | Negative |
| Gentle physical manipulation | Positive |
| Punishment | Negative |
| Behavior modification | Neutral |

## Requests and Commands

By virtue of common sense, we know that the first attempt to curb misbehavior should be a simple request: "Please stop doing that, okay?" Jamie, Drew's father, actually tried that when the boy first interrupted the conversation.

There's a right way to make a request, and most grandparents understand it instinctively. It's effective to ask in a soothing, melodious tone of voice rather than a threatening and demanding one. Use the cadence and tone of a question, with a rising inflection at the end: "Could I ask you to be quieter *please*?" In every human culture, we find that parents speak to their children in this manner to control their behavior. People are responsive to gentle, non-frightening approaches.

It's also true that making a request implies respect. We are asking someone to choose appropriate behavior rather than imposing it by force. This is highly important, because it gives the child responsibility for his or her behavior. Requests carry an implied cooperation between the adult and the child, yet the elder one's authority is in no way compromised or forfeited. As a matter of fact, most of us have greater respect for people who respect us; it is those who try to overpower us who tend to lose our respect.

As Jamie discovered, requests don't always succeed. Perhaps when a request doesn't result in success, a child is intent upon the behavior, or she is testing the limits. When she doesn't comply with the request, a command may be used. This, as the chart shows, is a more negative strategy, and that's why we ask nicely first. A command carries a stronger appeal to authority and power. It implies some sense of urgency in obedience. Commands are issued in a lower, more serious tone. What is significant is that a command shifts the burden to the one making the command, when obviously it's better for the child to be the one taking responsibility for wise choices.

Commands come in many forms: scolding, nagging, screaming and threatening, for example. Commands are more likely to work, but they come at the price of lessened effectiveness as parents or grandparents cooperating to help the child reach the goal of maturity. We all use commands at times, but the more we can avoid them, the better off we are.

*Pleasant but firm* is the correct approach. Threatening in any way draws your love into question, creating fear and, eventually, resentment in the child. Respect for your grandchild is incredibly important. It gives her a sense of dignity and self-worth, fills her emotional tank and teaches her how to relate to other people.

## Gentle Physical Manipulation

Particularly with younger children, and sometimes even with older ones, physical touch can be an effective way to solicit obedience. Try asking a two-year-old to come to you when she is busy playing. She will say, "No!" That word, of course, is the war cry of the two-year-old.

Try a request. "Child, would you please come see your grandfather?" *No!*

Use a command: "Child, come here right now, please." *No, no!*

Do you immediately impose punishment? "You will receive no dessert tonight!" I don't recommend that you punish so quickly. Instead, you take her by the arm and say, "Come along, child." Most of the time she will do so. Notice that this is one step past a command in power and authority. It is the use of force, but in a gentle and nonthreatening way. You've kept control of the situation, you've been firm, but you haven't raised your voice or created fear.

## WHEN TO PUNISH

What's the next alternative? Let's imagine that the child pulls away from you as you place your hand on her arm. Again she shouts her defiance, and perhaps runs away. The disobedience is now more serious and must be handled as such. You will have to move to the level of punishment, which is the most negative form of discipline, and which carries the highest risk.

One of the difficulties is that the grandparent must be wise enough to make the punishment fit the crime appropriately. Second, it must fit the age level, meaning that new variations of punishment must constantly be decided upon and applied. Third, we can never quite anticipate how a particular child will respond to punishment. What punishes one child may have little effect on another. And fourth, adults must be consistent in their application of punishment; it's so easy to act based on the adult's own level of frustration.

Yes, we're better off when we can avoid resorting to punishment, but I doubt there has ever been a parent or grandparent who could avoid having to do it at some point. We're not lying when we say, "This is going to hurt me more than it hurts you." Parents and grandparents alike agonize while their child is being punished. They wonder whether they're being too harsh; they fear that their children will have a burning resentment. They try to remember whether this punishment is consistent with warnings and precedents.

That's why it helps to do a little thinking beforehand. What are your grandchild's most common areas of misbehavior? What would be the most appropriate punishment, once you have exhausted lesser alternatives? What do the child's parents say about all this?

When the moment of misbehavior arrives, quickly ask yourself the series of questions we discussed above: *Is my grandchild's emotional tank full? Is the problem physical?* And so on. If all the answers are *no*, and you have no success with the other and more positive methods of behavior control, you need to ask, *Is my child actually being defiant?*

Defiance is openly resisting and challenging adult authority. It's certainly unacceptable in your home or in any other. Your task as a grandparent is to put down the rebellion without hurting the child's spirit in some way. Sometimes parents and grandparents overreact. They impose punishment out of proportion to the offense; then, when there is more serious misbehavior, they've overspent their "authority capital." This is why you need to be consistent and systematic by thinking things through in advance.

## THE QUESTION OF SPANKING

What approach did your parents take in the area of physical punishment? Those of us who are grandparents have seen the conventional wisdom come full circle in this area. Some of us were commanded to go break off our own hickory switches. Then, during the post-World War II generation, the influential Dr. Benjamin Spock urged parents to refrain from spanking. From 1970 on, however, there was an equal and opposite reaction, and some parents, particularly in conservative Christian circles, advocated more authoritarian approaches to parenting.

The answer usually lies somewhere in the middle. Even spanking has its positives along with its negatives. For instance, on the positive side, spanking does get results.

The negatives are equally obvious. The older a child grows, for example, the less effective physical punishment will be. Also, an angry parent who overuses physical punishment creates all the anger and resentment in the child that we've discussed throughout these chapters. Physical punishment plays into the hands of hot-tempered parents, and borders, in some cases, on abuse, which is a significant social issue in our time. On the practical side, some argue that spanking simply reinforces the idea of violence in children. It certainly does not model positive solutions for problems.

I once spoke to a man approaching his ninetieth birthday. Even at his advanced stage of life, he had not completely healed from the painful emotional scars of repeated spankings in his childhood. Yet, I'm always surprised to notice how many people practically boast about how often they were severely spanked as children. I believe that their parents must have deeply loved them and made them aware of it; otherwise they would not look upon their punishment as positively as they do.

Discipline is much riskier business in these times. Because there are so many negative cultural influences, and because parents themselves are struggling and children so often have special needs, the "good old-fashioned spanking" is much harder to package with love. Parents are living hectic lives and children have emptier emotional tanks; therefore, spankings tend to fit into patterns of perceived neglect by the children. Parents and grandparents need to think very hard before resorting to this area of punishment.

It's comforting to remember that discipline is not really about punishment, but about training the child in the way he should go (see Prov. 22:6). The more lovingly your grandchild is taught, the less punishment she needs.

There are times when we can effectively—and gently—use spanking as a last refuge. I observed a wonderful example a few years ago in the life of my granddaughter, Cami, who was only three at the time. Carey, my daughter, worked in the yard as Cami played.

My daughter had never spanked Cami up to this point. But the little girl was persistent in playing near the street. She was asked, then commanded, to play well back from the traffic. For whatever reason, my granddaughter was stubborn.

After the request and the command both failed, and Cami wandered into the street again, always watching her mother, Carey said firmly, "I warned you to stay out of the street, and I meant every word." And what do you think she did? Yes, she tried gentle physical manipulation, taking Cami's shoulder in her hands and leading her back to the safety of the front yard. I chuckled to myself: my daughter had been listening to her counselor of a father.

When Cami stepped into the street the next time, she received her first spanking. The message came through clearly, because when her daddy's car drove up, she called out, "Daddy! Don't run into the street!"

Don't agonize over this issue. In Cami's case, I can tell you that her parents did a wonderful job. Whether or not a child is spanked, that child can be loved, trained and guided toward emotional maturity and a successful adulthood. Fill the emotional tank and the issue will rarely arise.

## BEHAVIOR MODIFICATION

Earlier in the book we spoke of the "lab rat" technique of controlling behavior. Offer cheese for good behavior and a physical shock for bad behavior. During the middle of the twentieth century, scientists discovered how effective it could be. The mistake came when these insights were applied as a primary strategy for raising children. Obviously this would be a punishment-based and reactive way to approach misbehavior. It also teaches a very destructive lesson: A child will not receive unconditional love but love based strictly on her behavior.

I have seen young lives destroyed by this approach, for it leads to fear, resentment and eventually anger. Anything that undermines the atmosphere of unconditional love in a family is a terrible mistake. At the same time, even the reward module of behavior modification moves the child toward a selfish orientation: "What's in it for me?" If our children are taught to receive an all-A report card for monetary bonuses, for example, their love of learning is not enhanced. They simply learn to perform so that they can get what they want.

I believe that one of the chief reasons that values have steeply declined in our world is that a generation of children has been raised with behavior modification techniques. They have become adults concerned not with values and integrity, but with reward and penalty. They will do the right thing if they receive the right pay. And sometimes they discover that doing the wrong thing earns them some reward.

Therefore, we have a generational increase in income tax cheating and cutting corners in the quality of work. Lawyers become much more necessary because people won't do the right thing simply because it is right. We find that more of our kids are willing to cheat on tests—it's all about the consequence, and the consequence to them is the grade rather than the education.

Paul writes, "Let no debt remain outstanding, except the continuing debt to love one another" (Rom. 13:8). In the next verses, he explains that all the commandments are summarized in that Great Commandment, which is to love one another. All that we do in our homes should come from the heart rather than manipulation of any kind. How else will our children really know that we love them?

However, we can't rule out behavior modification techniques with children—not completely. I have always urged parents and grandparents to use this technique very cautiously and very rarely. You don't want your household to be a profit-driven business center, but a place of affection and loving relationships. There are certain times when rewards and penalties can be an effective approach without undermining the atmosphere of love. I strongly recommend Dr. Ruth Peters's book *Don't Be Afraid to Discipline.* The author is a behavioral psychologist who has a good and proper grasp of when behavior modification techniques can be used in a non-damaging way. We simply need to remember that a child's needs are primarily emotional, and the greatest need of all is unconditional love.

As a loving grandparent, you will find yourself drawn into this troubling question of discipline. It may be that you have to apply these principles personally as you care for the child in his or her parents' absence. Or it may be that you discover the lack of these principles in your adult child's parenting techniques. In that case, you are then bringing "discipline" to your adult child, in that you are guiding and training toward a better way. Fill your own child's emotional tank. Be gentle and loving in your suggestions that there could be a better way to deal with your grandchildren.

There is no higher calling in this world than the training of children. When you devote yourself to that cause, you are making a contribution to our world's future.

# 8

# The Protection Your Grandchild Craves

Ellen, a grandmother, had absolutely surprised herself. Somehow she had become an enthusiastic computer user. Who would have thought such a thing?

A decade or so ago, when computers seemed to explode onto the scene, she couldn't have been less enthusiastic. Why would anyone want a "personal computer"? She had been thrilled when videotape recorders first came out (she could tape her soap operas and watch them at her leisure). And she couldn't live without her microwave oven or even her cell phone. Ellen didn't feel she was *too* much of a technological refugee from the last century; she just hadn't foreseen that a computer could be so much fun.

But here she was, tapping away on a keyboard and seeing the words, in nice large print, on the monitor before her. A friend had talked her into taking a basic class at the Learning Annex, and now she knew her way around email, the Web and several important programs—including instant messaging. What a delight it had been to carry on an IM "conversation" with David, her 14-year-old grandson. At first, he couldn't believe his grandmother could become computer literate, much less take on the idiosyncrasies of Web chat. So he had gotten an extra kick out of saying hello to her over the Internet. Of course, she didn't want to make a nuisance of herself in his personal affairs, so she confined herself to the occasional "How's my grandson" email.

Then she had heard about the latest thing: "social networking." Her favorite TV talk show had a segment that told her all about it. Kids were creating their own personalized sections on certain websites that had names like MySpace and Facebook. They could post their digital photographs, leave each other messages, pass on information about movies they'd seen and bands they liked and keep their own Web logs ("blogs"). She understood: Certain sites were replacing the old burger joints as after-school hangouts for kids.

Ellen had heard David mention the particular site where he was active. She navigated to it on her Web browser and created an account of her own. Wouldn't he be surprised when his old-fashioned grandmother, straight from the days when dinosaurs walked the earth, appeared on his favorite networking site?

Ellen performed a name search and located her grandson—yes, that was his picture, all right. This was fun! She began to read his profile, and she could see the first few lines of messages that had been left for him by his friends.

Slowly the smile faded from Ellen's face. She could not believe some of the lines she was reading. Maybe this was "spam"—unsolicited Internet junk mail. Surely a fine young man such as David would have nothing to do with people like these. Each "friend" had a pictorial icon beside his or her name, and these certainly didn't look like wholesome young people. As for the words, they were laced with language much of which she had never even heard until she was an adult. She hung on to the hope that these were not really David's friends, or even that somehow this wasn't the same David.

Unfortunately, she couldn't ignore the evidence. The messages demonstrated that the young people did know the boy who was her grandson. There were references to his high school and favorite sports team. And some of the messages actually seemed to be parts of conversations David was actively having.

Ellen closed her Web browser's window with a sinking heart. She knew her David was growing up. He could not be a cute little third-grader forever, and adolescence is a strange time for any young person.

It certainly had been one for David's mother, whom Ellen had raised. But the things she had seen on David's Web page had startled her. The friends, language and hyperlinks suggested that David was part of a very dark, very rebellious culture. There was sexually suggestive wording, as if some of these 14-year-olds were already physically active in that area. There was a lot of casual talk about drunkenness and even drug use.

What was just as disturbing to Ellen was something intangible—it was just a general *tone* in which everything was written. She remembered that teenagers tend to use a lot of sarcasm, but the cynicism and down-on-everything language she had read on this website were truly scary. Surely many of these children came from fine, wholesome and church-going families, as David did. What would make them so negative, so bitter?

Ellen wondered how she could even face her grandson without feeling a little awkward—and what, if anything, should be said to David's parents?

Suddenly she wasn't so enthusiastic about the world of computers anymore. She didn't know if she was a refugee from the last century, but that time was looking pretty good all of a sudden.

## INTO THE WORLD

As we established at the beginning of this book, the times have changed, and not for the better. As a grandparent, you have the best view of all. You're the one who remembers the generations that preceded this one, and you've watched the slow erosion of traditional values and integrity. As I explained in the first chapter, I believe that most grandparents aren't aware of just how radical these changes are—Ellen would be a good example. Still, I'm certain you would agree that a child of today lives in a totally different social environment than a child of 40 years ago.

When does the impact on our children become a primary concern? For the most part, we must be on our guard as late childhood moves into early adolescence. This is when the structure of your grandchild's life begins to change. The world of a younger child is dominated by parents, particularly the mother. We've discussed those "helicopter" parents who hover over their preschool- and early elementary-age children. They have the ability to determine what television shows, books, people and experiences their children may encounter. That's such a wonderful and crucial period as your grandchild formulates values, talents and the ability to make decisions.

But the helicopter can only follow so far. The influence of the parent moves from total to partial as the child begins to grow. As a teenager, peers loom ever larger in importance. But there are things that you and the parents can do to help the child. For example, you as a grandparent might make it financially possible to send the child to a private school, where the educational quality might be higher than at a public school. Many parents today are coming to the conclusion that this is a necessary step. Unfortunately, too many of them have other priorities. They are driving more expensive cars or taking on higher mortgage payments. My plea to the parents themselves is this: Please let your child and his education be your very highest calling! Perhaps the public schools are excellent in your community. But you need to be certain about that; if they're not excellent, you need to find superior options.

Again, grandparents can make the difference. In many cases, grandparents have the ability to lend financial assistance to their children for such purposes.

Home schooling, of course, is another option. I would love to see more grandparents (assuming they have the required health, time and location) provide hope in this area. Yes, it's a tremendous commitment that would take a great deal of thought. You would need to sacrifice several hours a day in working with one or more children. But I can't imagine a greater legacy to leave for the future. And what a wonderful way to spend time with your grandchildren! Of course, this won't be possible for a grandparent who lives at a distance, or one still in the work force. But perhaps a few readers have a new idea to consider.

This chapter is about security and protection for our precious grandchildren. How can we possibly take care of that goal when we have such a limited amount of time with them?

The answer, of course, is that we teach them to be young men and women of clear minds, godly spirit and strong integrity.

## Innocent but Shrewd

There are certain things we can do while our grandchildren are young.

We can surround them with unconditional love, wise discipline, lessons in anger management and wholesome cultural media for their early years. We can send them to worthy public schools, superior private ones or consider home schooling. We can be certain that they attend the finest churches with the best programs for young people. Sooner or later, they will still have to stand on their own two feet within this world. They will have to leave the cloister and make decisions without Mom, Dad or the loving grandparents. What will they make of that opportunity? Will we be proud, or will be afraid to make the kind of discovery that Ellen made?

I want to assure you that there's good reason for hope, no matter what poor influences may surround your grandchild. For one thing, an emotional tank kept full throughout those early years will make a difference. Your grandchild will know what it's like to be unconditionally loved and accepted. He will be deeply influenced by the values of the elders who raised him. I look around today and I see many young people who have clearly been raised by outstanding parents, and they will continue making their parents and grandparents proud. So many of them are already lighting a candle rather than cursing the darkness of this world. Even for Ellen's grandson, there are so many good things that can be done to help David develop as the person they want him to be.

Trust God to watch over the family you love. Trust Him to provide the love, power and security for your grandchildren. Psalm 127 begins, "Unless the LORD builds the house, its builders labor in vain." The psalmist creates a word picture of our children and grandchildren as arrows in the warrior's quiver:

Blessed is the man
whose quiver is full of them.
They will not be put to shame
when they contend with their enemies in the gate (v. 5).

Think of that image. You are an archer with long-range influence. You set your sights with care, draw back the bowstring with all your strength and fire those arrows (your beloved children and grandchildren) into an always-uncertain future. Our children are the world's best hope for a peaceful and positive world tomorrow.

The archer, of course, must aim with precision and care. The arrows themselves must be fashioned and polished with excellence. Parents and grandparents alike must realize there is nothing in the world more important than protecting and securing our children from the harmful influences that are all around us. That means we must learn to think in a new way. We can't just take it for granted that schoolteachers will impart the basic lessons we want imparted. We can't simply assume that the children up the street, with whom our grandchild plays, are appropriate companions.

Jesus sent out His disciples with these words: "I am sending you out like sheep among wolves. Therefore be as shrewd as snakes and as innocent as doves" (Matt. 10:16). I've always been fascinated by those words, which seem to ring more true as each year passes. To me, they mean that we need to be shrewd and savvy in the ways of the world, and help our children be likewise. Innocence is one thing, but naïveté is dangerous.

Jesus tells us it's possible to be innocent and still be wise. Ellen, having gotten a taste of her grandson's world, wanted to retreat into a nostalgic comfort zone. Of course, that's not the answer. Forewarned is forearmed. Let's know where the dangers lie so that we can help protect our grandchildren from harmful influences.

## Learning to Think

Based upon my observations over the years, I believe that age 17 is a golden year. By that time your grandchild has the opportunity to be adept at managing anger and to know how to make mature decisions. I think a fully developed conscience and value system can be in place by that age.

During the childhood and adolescent years that precede that point, you have an opportunity to help your grandchild learn to think wisely. There are so many more opportunities to do that than you might believe. For instance, your children and grandchildren might have come for a visit, and you might be sitting together in the family room discussing local or national events. Be conscious of whether younger ears are listening. Take that opportunity to talk about what is right and wrong—and why it is so. Let your grandchildren hear you evaluate the world and its ways based upon sound biblical and ethical considerations.

Perhaps you will watch a television show or a movie together. I know that you'll watch appropriate programs as a family, but there might still be times when you can ask, "What do you think about this character's decision? Would you have done the same?" It's possible to demonstrate the difference it makes when we apply our Christian beliefs to the issues that confront us in culture.

Let's imagine that you're reading the paper and you come across an article about how many young people illegally download and share popular songs over the Internet. This is now a completely common practice even among Christian young people. You tear out the article, clip it to your refrigerator door and raise the conversation topic when your grandchild is visiting. "This article is interesting," you say. "I had no idea that the music industry is in trouble due to illegal file sharing. What's your opinion about that?"

Notice the soft, non-accusatory way of raising the question. Your role is not to play "I caught you!" with your grandchild, but to help him learn to think biblically. As you gently discuss the topic, you could mention the Bible's commandment not to steal (see Exodus 20:15). Then you could talk about the perfectly sensible reasons why God sets boundaries for His children. He does so, of course, out of love. He wants us to protect and honor each other. We can teach them chapter and verse, but the real lessons are about how to think for ourselves.

Judges 21:25 describes a time very much like our modern days. Israel lacked moral leadership, and therefore, "everyone did what was right in his own eyes" (*NKJV*). Wouldn't it be an enlightening conversation if you asked your grandchild what he sees at school or in his social life that fits that verse? If you and his parents don't teach him to do what is right in God's eyes, he will live exactly as the world teaches him.

I believe that now, more than ever, integrity is a central issue. All around us we see the lack of it. Not only do our leaders fall short in this area—they are the very ones who lack it the most. I want my grandchildren to understand what a young man or a young woman of integrity is. Let me share with you the three traits I'm talking about:

1. Telling the truth
2. Keeping promises
3. Taking responsibility for one's behavior

I invite you to think carefully about your grandchildren and how they're learning each of these cornerstone values.

## Telling the Truth

In recent years, we've seen the spectacle of an American president placing his hand on a Bible, taking an oath and swearing to tell the truth, the whole truth and nothing but the truth—then lying. When it became clear that he had prevaricated (and admitted such), there were many voices in the media who found no fault with our nation's leader lying under oath—not to mention the sexual act that his lie attempted to cover up. Many people made the claim that it's all right to lie to protect one's family from embarrassment.

Current events can be used to train your grandchild. (Obviously there were elements of that news event that would be inappropriate to discuss with young children.) "What might happen," you can ask, "if everyone steals or fails to tell the truth? How would it affect your life if you knew that your closest friends might be lying to you at any time?"

A few years ago, I read a survey that showed that a shocking number of American workers had called in sick while perfectly healthy, stolen office supplies, lied on résumés and lied to their spouses about important issues. Honesty is the bottom line of any relationship. When we lose that basic trust, we can accomplish almost nothing together. Note the effect of dishonesty on many marriages.

What are the honesty issues in the life of your grandchild? Be observant. Ask questions. Has he ever caught a friend in a lie? How did that make him feel? This is an important area in which to train your beloved grandchild.

## Keeping Promises

Have you noticed how the value of a commitment is almost nil today? I noticed a story about college football recently. The coaches, who are role models for their players, often opt out of contracts for all kinds of reasons. A school awards them a guaranteed contract for five years of service and pays them well; but a coach has a big year, gets a better offer and finds a way out. Meanwhile, he recruits players who make verbal "commitments" to attend that college; next week, the player takes back his "commitment" and makes another "commitment" to go somewhere else.

Is it any wonder? We have few role models today when it comes to keeping promises. We all know that most of our leaders stand before God and their loved ones in a church, promising to honor and keep their marriage vows until death parts the two of them. Yet among our leaders, I would guess that the divorce rate is much higher than the 50 percent level it attains in the general public.

When I call a plumber, he says he will come tomorrow; when he doesn't show up, I'm no longer surprised. If someone tells me the check is in the mail, I have reason to doubt his word. Just the area of returning a phone call is an epidemic of broken promises.

Grandparent, do you stand by your word? When you make a commitment, do you feel bound by honor to keep it? This is an absolutely urgent area for teaching our youth. What happens if your grandson promises to clean his room in exchange for early allowance, then doesn't keep his side of the bargain? What are the consequences if he learns that it's really not important to be honor-bound?

As I write, we have a national crisis in mortgage default. Declaring bankruptcy is now just another financial strategy by which someone gets a do-over without any responsibility of paying down a debt. In just a short number of years, this could be your grandchild. We all make mistakes, but the real problem is that people believe they can do so without consequences. What would be the positive effect on our legal system—and our national economy—if a sizeable number of people simply began keeping their word?

What if your grandson has a baby-sitting commitment, and something more exciting comes along? Discuss that scenario with him. Ask him what issues of character and honor might be involved. Teach him a lesson about the power of personal commitment.

## Taking Responsibility

In human history, it took almost no time at all for us to develop the problem of not taking responsibility. After the first sin in world history, God confronted Adam, who replied, "The woman you put here with me—she gave me some fruit from the tree" (Gen. 3:12).

God looked to Eve, and her story was this: "The serpent deceived me" (v. 13).

Nowadays, if someone commits a crime, it is likely to be the fault of "society," one's parents or anyone else but the person in the mirror. Some of us are old enough to remember the plaque that sat on the desk of President Harry Truman: "The Buck Stops Here." Today the "buck" doesn't stop, but keeps laying itself at someone else's feet.

We all know that children have always been experts at pointing the finger and saying, "He started it!" The problem, once again, is that adult role models have done a poor job of presenting a mature alternative in recent years. When parents come home and blame other people for their problems, young people hear. They can't help but think that if the blame game works so well for adults, why shouldn't it work for them?

Personal injury lawsuits have become an American phenomenon. People have actually sued fast-food restaurants, holding the establishments responsible for making them obese. Our U.S. Congress had to spend valuable time writing a bill to throw out such frivolous lawsuits. Have your grandchildren ever heard their parents or grandparents say, "This is my fault. I take full responsibility"?

Our goal is for grandchildren to step up and take ownership of their lives, their decisions and their mistakes. Can you model such values for your grandchild?

How do we make these values take root in them?

## HELPING THEM VALUE YOUR VALUES

Every child needs to learn to clearly think through decisions. As I've explained in a previous chapter, so many of our personal decisions and reactions have to do with unconscious emotions. That's simply normal human behavior. However, we can also say that the more crystal-clear a person is in his thinking, and the more he decides and acts based upon principles (and the right ones), the more emotionally mature he will be.

Someday, when they are adults, your grandchildren will remember you and particularly the ways you thought and acted. They will recognize that their grandparents were touchstones to another time and to values that they will come to value themselves. Don't you feel that way about your own grandparents? The older we become, the more we respect them and the forces that molded them. Therefore, look upon the present as a time to take charge of the memories with which you leave your grandchildren.

Underline your thinking processes to them so that they can see that your thoughts were molded by your faith and the good common sense that God gave you. When you find grandchildren thinking unclearly, or with undue bias, as children will do, gently show them the way to disentangle their poor logic and make better evaluations. Let me share some practical ways that you can do that.

### Use I-messages to Make a Point

Let's return to the discussion of illegal music downloads, which would be an issue that would resonate with so many young people today. Here is how one grandparent might discuss the issue: "Do you download songs without paying for them? It's breaking the law and it's a sin!"

That's an example in which you have a very strong point to make, but you also have a good chance of losing your audience. As right as you are, your dictatorial style will not lubricate the message to go down any easier. An I-message would go something like this: "I worry about those illegal downloads because they deprive the artists of money their talent and hard work has earned. I also tend to ask myself whether God would want me to do something like that." You've presented your own opinion—an approach that is less confrontational. You've also made a *because* statement; young people want to be given sound, practical reasons. And rather than making a demand, you've left the issue for the young person (a teenager) to decide for himself. Ultimately that's what he will have to do.

If your grandchild disagrees, he will feel free to discuss his opinions with you in an open way. When we treat our grandchildren with respect, we have much better opportunities to train them. Quite often they will indeed present an alternative view, but you can lovingly and likeably offer your thinking on the matter. He may not admit it, but he is being taught and influenced even if he doesn't immediately agree with what he has heard. Your thoughts will go with him when he leaves.

## Let Your Grandchildren Do Their Own Thinking

Oh, how tempted we are to simply give the right answers! We want to jump right in with our opinions, solving the puzzle for someone else in the room.

Have you ever listened as someone related a problem she was experiencing, only to discover that she wasn't asking for your advice? What she wanted was a listening ear as she worked it out for herself. She was doing the right thing, and if you listened quietly, so were you. People grow when they take responsibility for solving their own problems; our help can actually hinder if we short-circuit another person's thinking processes.

Immature people (that is, children) will make immature remarks. Please avoid the impulse to make harsh corrections or straight-out contradictions. Your goal is to gently, patiently beckon to that young mind to move toward an alternative solution that is a more mature one. When teenagers in particular feel that their ideas will be ridiculed or disrespected in some way, they decide not to speak at all. Then we lose any opportunity to help them, other than hoping they will listen as we speak to others.

Grandmother Ellen did a very nice job of using these concepts. She thought and prayed about how to deal with her knowledge of David's life on the social networking website. She finally decided not to embarrass her grandchild by "visiting" him on the site, but to raise the conversational point with him privately. One day, when the two of them were together, she mentioned that she had heard a lot about social networking sites. Did David enjoy using them?

He replied that he did. His grandmother asked him what kind of place it was, in his experience. Did he find it a positive destination for hanging out? Were there some dangers, as she understood there were?

David began to talk a bit more about his experiences. After all, he knew his grandmother was an easy person to talk to, always interested and never accusatory. He admitted to her that she probably would be shocked by some of the things she would see there. He gave some examples, though he was very cautious about what he shared. Ellen continued to express interest and ask questions, slowly encouraging David to be more transparent. Eventually he admitted that it was easy to get caught up in some of the language and inappropriate subject matter that was on this site. He said, "I don't use a lot of bad words, but it seems like my friends get more and more raunchy, and they talk about stuff that makes me feel awkward. I guess sometimes I follow the crowd a little too."

His grandmother asked, "What is that like? How do you feel when you go along with the crowd?"

David was quiet for a moment. He said, "Sort of guilty, I guess."

Ellen gave him a little hug and said, "That's why you're special, dear grandson. God gave you a conscience, didn't He?"

"I guess maybe so. I didn't think about that."

"So do you think you'll keep using those sites?"

"I would say, not so much. Actually I think I would get in trouble if Mom saw some of the stuff there."

Ellen could tell that David was surprised by his own honesty. She waited a few days, talked about it again with David, then quietly informed David's parents about the conversation. She told them, "I want you to know that you are doing a great job with David. He made the right decision all on his own, despite peer pressure. But if you tell him I mentioned all this, he will never confide in me again." Before she took this step, she knew she could trust the parents.

## TIMING IS EVERYTHING

I want to make one final point about teaching our grandchildren to think clearly so that they'll be protected from the onslaught of a post-Christian culture. In teaching, timing is all-important. Some people call this the "teachable moment."

As an example, you might be worried about the friends your grandchild has. You may want to talk to him about peer pressure. But when you raise the subject, you may get a glassy stare in return. For your grandson, that issue simply isn't a burning one for the time being.

Several days later, however, you might hear about a case where a local youth experienced a tragic drug overdose. Your grandchild might hear the same story and would then be interested in discussing it with you; the teachable moment has come. If you're a wise, prepared grandparent, you might have gathered more information about what happened, and you may even have a brochure or a collection of Internet information on the problem of peer pressure that caused the youth to get involved with drugs.

Loving adult guardians always have one eye on the child and one eye on the dynamics of the moment. What is going on right now emotionally? What opportune lesson has presented itself? There are two particular moments you should watch out for:

1. *When your grandchild brings you a question.* You know the path is clear for teaching when your grandchild initiates the conversation. It could be a question about life when you were a child, for example. It could be curiosity about your opinion on some subject. Younger children, as we all know, are full of questions. Some adults, even some grandparents, become annoyed by the barrage. They don't realize the wonderful opportunity they have for making an impression on an open mind.

2. *When you are connecting emotionally.* There are those moments when we feel very close to our grandchildren. Again, for the little ones, bedtime is an example. They will listen to what either a parent or a grandparent has to say at such a time. They're about to be alone in the dark, and they instinctively realize they need their emotional tanks filled for the nighttime journey. As I've said frequently, filling the tank is the best way to create a teachable attitude. When you enjoy such a moment together, ask questions: *What are you happiest about right now? What would make tomorrow a perfect day?* Initiate thinking, reflecting and dreaming. You're enhancing the loving relationship that you have together, and you're seeding a young spirit for guidance and training.

At those moments, when you feel particularly close, you realize just how deeply you feel about this young person. You remember just how difficult a world it is, and you want your grandchild to be secure and safeguarded. You know that when you go to sleep tonight, you'll pray for this precious soul and his future. You'll ask God to care for him when you're no longer able to do so, and that He will use your grandchild in a special way in this world.

And of course, you'll thank God for the opportunity you've had—the chance to have a part in firing a wonderful arrow into the future of this world. You know that there is no darkness so deep that God's light will not penetrate it. This is a bright young life, and you have this opportunity to help him shine.

That thought gives you hope for tomorrow, and then you, too, will sleep well.

# 9

# The Special Needs of Your Grandchild

Honestly, I think you're making a mountain of a molehill," said Alice to her daughter. "Children just have a lot of energy. Sometimes they're restless, that's all. You were the same way, and we didn't need a fancy alphabetical label to describe it—what was that label again, ACDC?"

"ADHD," replied Anna. "Attention-Deficit Hyperactivity Disorder, Mom. It's very real. We just didn't know much about these things when I was growing up, or when you were a child." The two of them were clearing the table after a family meal. Alice had come to stay with her daughter, son-in-law and grandchild for a few days.

"Whatever you say, dear," Alice replied. "All I know is that we've managed to raise pretty good children all these years without this—this psychobabble that everybody uses these days. We just did it the old-fashioned way instead of popping some new pill into them every five minutes. I don't see why my baby has to be on some kind of drug to go to third grade."

"It's called Adderal, Mom, and it's doctor-prescribed. It just helps to regulate some of the chemical activities in Lissa's brain so that she is calm and clear in the morning when she needs to be. Don't you remember how she wouldn't stay in a chair in her first-grade class? She would just get up and roam, and the teacher couldn't manage her. Bless her heart, the child couldn't help herself."

"I think it was just because she's bursting with personality," said Alice. "She's a free spirit. She comes by it naturally."

"Well, the problem is that she couldn't get anything done that way, and neither could anyone else," said Anna patiently. "Believe me, we wanted to be very careful with Lissa. We wouldn't let her go on some medication if we hadn't checked out all the facts very closely. I've explained all that to you, Mom."

"I know, I know," said Alice as she ran a sponge across the counter. "It's just that it all seems so strange to me. I don't know why everything has to be so different. My Lissa seems so normal, so adorable to me. Saturday morning we sat down together and read a story, and she was so bright, so attentive . . ."

"It was morning and she'd had her pill, Mom. Don't you see? It really helped her sit down with you and focus on the story. The prescription medication helped her be who she really is, without all the interference of an attention deficit. Sort of like a TV that can now stay on one channel for an entire episode instead of switching around to all those other channels on its own."

"Oh, I hate that on a television!" laughed Alice. "I want to grab that remote out of your husband's hand. Can't we give him a pill?"

## A New Day with New Needs

Where did all this come from? All of these new needs and new prescriptions? Isn't a child still a child anymore, or does she have to come with some kind of fancy "disorder"?

Our grandchildren are perfect in every way—just like our children were. We carry around all their photographs to show and brag about to friends. We keep their artwork on our refrigerators, and we glow with pride just to think about them. Then there suddenly arises this question of a "behavioral disorder," or some other kind of "special need."

Why shouldn't we be skeptical? All of these terms seem to be new inventions. We didn't hear about eating disorders and adolescent depression and learning disabilities in the good old days. Couldn't this just be the psychiatric and pharmaceutical industries finding a new way to make a buck?

The truth is that behavioral disorders have always been around. We just recognize them more clearly, and it is really the labels and some of the prescriptive medicines that are new. As I read through history, I often smile when I recognize signs of ADHD in some of our most creative thinkers, leaders and artists. I've counseled parents who were distressed to learn that their child might have a four-initial "disorder." So I talked to them about Kit Carson, who was a frontier leader in the 1800s. He was well loved by Native Americans and Spanish-Americans because he was simply a good person. I read several biographies of him before finally coming to his much less popular autobiography. That, along with the notes and letters in his museum, showed me that he clearly had ADHD. Even his penmanship showed the unmistakable symptoms.

Highly creative and original people have always been more prone to having ADD or ADHD. There simply wasn't a name for it in earlier times.

At the same time, however, with many other disorders, we quickly recognize why they are on the upswing. Our times are filled with fear and anxiety. There are more young people from unstable homes; there is violence in schools, fears about the environment and the future, and so many more issues to challenge a young person and her emotional growth.

That's why it's so crucial for every parent to be aware of the danger signals and the available resources for treatment. There should be no stigma in identifying a special challenge, whether it's a learning disability, an eating disorder or some other issue. These are all symptoms of being human in an extraordinary world.

Finally, just being a young person is challenging enough. Surely you can remember the turmoil of being a teenager. It's the most topsy-turvy era of life, because on the one end we are children, while on the other, we are adults. The transition is never too easy—and making it in today's culture is harder than ever.

If a grandchild of any age has a special need of some kind, it doesn't reflect on her parents or her grandparents. The most wonderful and outstanding homes face these challenges. We can't afford to look upon these things as affronts to our personal pride or as fabrications of medical culture. Instead, let's look clearly and objectively at our grandchildren, diagnose their true needs and lovingly give them the help and guidance they need. My hope and prayer are that this chapter will help any grandparent do that.

## FACING FEAR AND ANXIETY

What things scare a child? How about a teenager?

We all know that fear is a normal part of childhood. What little one hasn't gone through a period of anxiety when the lights were turned off and it seemed that some monster must have taken residence in the closet? Children can be afraid of darkness, strangers, water, riding a bicycle, or of nearly anything else. When we are so young, nearly everything in life is new. Every day brings some fresh change or challenge. And that's what fear is: the body's natural aversion to the unknown.

As we reach a new age and stage, of course, our fears change. They are more subtle and difficult to see—in the eyes of others as well as ourselves. All children fear the loss of love and security; that's why this book includes chapters on how grandparents can be sure to supply them. There are more changes during the years of adolescence than at any other time. A teenager is pushed from the comfort zone, a secure world of parental protection, into a place where she must ensure her own protection.

What can a grandparent do? You can provide the comfort of permanence and stability. So much is constantly changing in the lives of our children. Every year is utterly unlike the one before it. The world itself seems unreliable and unfriendly, because, by and large, it is. I believe parents today are so absorbed by the challenges of career life that they often fail to provide that sense of security that children crave. We need grandparents to stand in the gap, providing extra love and emotional support to both children and grandchildren. When you are with your grandchild, be conscious of her emotions. She will see in you a trusted adult who has moved through many of the storms of life and emerged victorious. Therefore, she'll listen to the wisdom and encouragement you have to offer.

Watch for anxiety as well. Many children suffer from an excessive amount of it today. Anxiety is an insidious form of fear, because it's characterized by the lack of awareness of what we fear. One character in an old comic strip had an "anxiety closet." It was filled with all the nameless dreads and worries, all of which were hidden behind that closed door. That's the way it is with anxiety; when we bring our worries out into the light, so to speak, we nearly always discover they're not nearly as large or formidable as we suspected. Have you ever suffered from anxiety? What situations in life made you anxious?

One pervasive form of anxiety is *stress*, a mental or emotional strain brought on by the prospect of change. When we face an unreasonable number of changes at any time in life, we become stressed, or we say that we are in *distress*.

When stress and anxiety become issues, we have an opportunity to show our grandchildren how faith actually works in the problems of life. Every Christian should know and use the following verse from Paul, who wrote it while he was under arrest and facing execution by the Romans:

> Do not be anxious about anything, but in everything, by prayer and petition, with thanksgiving, present your requests to God. And the peace of God, which transcends all understanding, will guard your hearts and your minds in Christ Jesus (Phil. 4:6-7).

These are more than soothing words. They are a promise from the creator of the universe that we can bring Him our worries, and He will bring us His peace. Paul gives us the word picture of a guard, posting a sentry around our hearts and minds during the night watch. Do you personally take advantage of that promise? Can you show your grandchild a model of how to be strong in a world of fear and stress?

Of course, a grandparent may not hear about the child's items of anxiety. Many times these concerns aren't even shared with the parents these days. You must create a relationship that will make a child more likely to come and confide in you. Be as familiar as you can be with her world. Pick up the clues that she might drop even when she can't or won't verbalize what is bothering her. There will be times when you may actually have a better chance to discern the problem than the child, because many younger people aren't able to identify just what issues are entwining in their lives to bring about the stress.

As always, our number-one rule is to keep your grandchild's emotional tank full. Encourage her parents to make sure she feels loved and accepted. Think about your own emotions when you feel fear or anxiety. It always helps to know that someone loves you, supports you and prays for you. Teenagers in particular tend to feel insecure. They're still working out who they are and where they fit in this world, and the all-important network of their peers can be frustrating and turbulent. A teenage boy looks into the mirror and sees acne. A teenage girl is adjusting to the disturbing new world of her menstrual cycle. More than teenagers consciously realize, they want that love and security that comes from the primary and extended family.

What if a young person doesn't find the loving nurture she needs during her hour of doubt? She won't learn the lesson of love. The maturation of her own emotions will be stunted, so that as an adult she'll struggle to give and receive love. None of us can give what we ourselves have not received.

But if you're constantly maintaining a foundation of unconditional love for your grandchild, she will feel better and more confident. Her anxiety is more likely to be under control.

## CHILDREN AND DEPRESSION

During the last few decades we've seen early depression rise to a level of epidemic proportion. It's particularly prevalent in teenagers (one in eight suffers from it, according to some accounts). Experts tell us that parents are missing the key signals. Depression can be very subtle, taking forms we don't recognize. It's not too surprising that adults often don't realize what their children are experiencing emotionally. A serious problem in this area is known as clinical depression. You can learn to watch out for its signs so that your grandchild receives the help she needs.

Those of us who are grandparents were raised in different times. We spoke of "moodiness" and "the blues," and certainly there are times when people simply have low spirits as a brief and passing phase. But true depression can't be shrugged off. It's a serious problem, and studies show that young people who develop it are three to four times more likely than their peers to experience problems with substance abuse by their mid-twenties. It's also true that teenage suicide has been on the increase, quadrupling in frequency in half a century's time.

All of this is true, but parents and grandparents who seriously follow the basics of parenting—providing unconditional love and protection, teaching anger management, guiding a child through sound discipline—are at far less risk to experience these problems with their children. So don't be alarmed; simply be observant when you're with your grandchild.

What kind of behaviors should catch your attention? Severe anxiety, for one. It is the most frequent precursor of teenage depression. If your grandchild seems to have a world of worries and is very difficult to reassure, she is at risk for depression.

Here are some other traits of depressed children:

- They are often children of divorce or marital discord.
- They seem to be less socially adept; they either receive or imagine rejection, and are therefore shy and withdrawn.
- They suffer from poor self-image, connecting their problems to perceived personal flaws, as opposed to temporary or changeable behavior.
- They experience great amounts of stress.
- They suffer from shorter attention spans and struggle to complete goals.

Take your grandchild's gender into consideration, for boys and girls have different ways of manifesting their depression. Girls may be more transparent with their emotions, so that in their case, we have a slightly better chance of catching on to the problem. While girls are more passive in their anxiety, boys are more active. A depressed teenage boy may be aggressive to peers, and he may have brushes with the law. We don't tend to associate aggression with depression, and therefore we can miss the true problem.

The age of 11 seems to be the time when depression may set in for girls. There is a 4-year window from 11 to 15 when girls are more likely to experience some level of it. Needless to say, this is a time of great biological change for them. Socially, they're adjusting from being little girls to becoming young women. They tend to reflect more on their problems than boys do. They brood about their appearance, their families, their popularity and their possessions. Because we train girls to be more sensitive and caring, they feel things more deeply as well.

We must also guard against the danger of treating symptoms rather than the true problem. If your granddaughter was discovered abusing drugs, you would be so disturbed that you might address the drug issue first, failing to consider whether depression was the true cause. The only genuine way to deal with the girl's situation would be to treat the depression, after which the drug problem would take care of itself. But many parents and guardians would tend to focus on the narcotic angle.

Depression approaches stealthily rather than suddenly. We watch for lifestyle changes, such as a drop in grades. This would be an example of the vicious cycle of depression: She is depressed, therefore her grades drop; therefore she is more depressed. Treating the symptom would never work.

I always recommend that parents and grandparents keep their children in a wholesome atmosphere as much as possible. Young people have developed strikingly dark cultures of music, fashion and video games, and these are entirely wrong places for young people to congregate, particularly when they are at high risk of suffering from depression. Most high schools today have subcultures with names such as "goth" or "emo" that all but formalize adolescent negativism, with dark clothing, cynical outlooks and dead-end futures. Do all that you can to help your grandchild move in more positive circles. Church youth activities should be encouraged, and outdoor recreation is therapeutic for teenage depression.

## Signs of Depression

We're talking primarily about teenagers here. If your grandchild displays *not one, but several* of these symptoms, you should consider consultation and counseling.

Watch for feelings of sadness, hopelessness, despair, lack of purpose or lack of interest in activities that brought pleasure in the past.

Watch for short attention span and an inability to concentrate or make a decision.

Watch for inattention to personal hygiene.

Watch for the decision to quit scouts, clubs, youth group, team sports, music.

Watch for a rapid plummet in academic performance.

Watch for extreme amounts of time spent alone.

Watch for physical symptoms: persistent aching, either muscular or common headaches; lack of energy; a rapid increase or decrease in appetite; weight changes; inability to sleep, or the desire to sleep too often.

Watch for unpredictable moods: irritability, anxiety, surly disposition or frequent disputes with others.

Talk to teachers, coaches, and youth leaders. Have they seen behavior changes?

This can be a touchy matter, and we want to be cautious without overreacting. We know that teenagers like time alone—this in itself is not a sign of depression. Adolescents use a lot of sarcasm in their speech, so that in itself would not be a reason to begin worrying. But do look for a *cluster* of symptoms.

## LEVELS OF DEPRESSION

There are many grades of depression. Sometimes depression is quite mild and we can easily manage the symptoms and causes. If we do a good job, the depression will not grow to be a greater and deeper problem. Parents and grandparents simply need to be aware of what is going on in the child's life, and be aware of what to look out for in terms of depression indicators.

Be especially watchful during times of transition. Obviously a period of marital problems for the parents would be rough for the child. So would a physical move to a new neighborhood or school. All children thrive in a stable and secure atmosphere, and the more turbulent life becomes, the more stress and anxiety the child will face.

Do you have a college-age grandchild? I remember talking to some friends of our daughter Carey when they were away at school. I was struck by how homesick many of them were. These older adolescents expressed a deep longing to receive phone calls and letters from their family and friends. Probably every one of them had a grandparent who assumed that the child was leading a life of fun and excitement in the college atmosphere.

It's also true that the beginning of college is the most likely time for a child's parents to divorce; they figure they can finally separate, now that their child is out of the home. Imagine what it's like, however, to be homesick and know that the "home" is vanishing forever. This is going to continue to be the way of the world, sadly enough. But you can see what a difference a grandparent could make in that situation. Once again, the grandparent is a symbol of stability and security.

If your grandchild suffers from moderate or severe depression, she may lose some of her ability to think clearly, logically and rationally. The area of hurting will become the lens for interpreting everything else in her life. Her world becomes a gray and hopeless landscape. As a counselor, I have trouble working with such a young person because she isn't reason-oriented during this time. Those who love her must love her more powerfully and actively than ever before, so that she won't act out her depression in some way. Depression will not fade away on its own.

## A WORD ABOUT DEPENDENT OR SHY CHILDREN

One category that may or may not be related to depression, depending upon the example, is the category of those grandchildren who are especially shy or dependent upon their parents. There are many children that fit this profile today.

First, we need to realize that these young ones are at risk for depression, either now or later. Look upon it as an amber "caution light" to be extra sensitive to the emotional needs of the child and to deal with the depression if other symptoms develop over time. However, extreme shyness or dependency does not absolutely suggest a diagnosis of depression. We've all known shy people, particularly children. Sometimes it is a normal stage of development and growth. Today's painfully bashful early adolescent may emerge as an extroverted young adult.

As grandparents, we find yet another golden opportunity to make a difference. If a child clings to the mother's apron strings, terrified of anyone she doesn't know, then we can offer the chance to venture out and interact with the "next safest adult." Beyond the parents themselves, grandparents are the most likely adults to be loved and trusted by a child. If your grandchild is shy, therefore, make a special point to spend time with her. Help her slowly and comfortably learn that life need not be terrifying and can even be stimulating when the parents are not around. This can become a crucial step in learning how to interact with others outside the home.

## EATING DISORDERS

Eating disorders often trouble young women between the ages of 12 and 25. Young ladies begin to feel the pressure to be the "perfect" woman that our celebrity-obsessed culture demands them to be. There is a preoccupation with waist size and an impossible bodily perfection that inevitably leads to very unhealthy behaviors. Let's consider a few of these.

- *Anorexia nervosa* involves a refusal to maintain a minimally normal body weight. Another word for it could be *starvation*. Severe anorexia is life threatening. You may remember the popular singer Karen Carpenter, whose health problems spiraled out of control because of this disorder. It led to her tragic death.

- *Bulimia nervosa* is the number-one eating disorder among young women. Binge eating, followed by purging the body of food or of weight gain, characterize this one. The danger here is that we can't go on physical appearances; it's possible to have a normal weight and waistline, and still suffer from bulimia.

- *Binge eating disorder* involves overeating, without purging, on a frequent basis. Males make up a higher percentage of this disorder, but large numbers of young women have reported taking a "binging" approach to their eating at some time or other.

Grandparents, you cannot over-love or over-nurture these children. We must help them understand that they are perfect just as God made them; they need not conform to some unrealistic image of the swimsuit model. We love them, and people will love them too, because of who they are. The child's self-concept is all-important. If she knows that she is special, that she is intelligent and attractive simply because God created her and loves her, she will be far less likely to chase after the mirage of bodily perfection.

We need to reclaim the biblical image of the body. It is God's holy temple, not a runway for fashion models. The bodily temple is all about glorifying God, but it is His presence, rather than the workmanship of the building, that makes it special. God has a plan for your granddaughter, and she need not worry, overeat or under-eat herself into a dangerous state in some desperate pursuit of becoming someone else. Help her to trust God and to love the way that He has created her.

At the same time, maybe we grandparents should reassess our own relationship to food. Whenever the family comes over, we love to eat. The dinner table is a joyful place for family fellowship. It wouldn't hurt for us to model healthy eating and good dietary habits.

# ADD AND ADHD

By now, nearly everyone has heard about Attention-Deficit Disorder (ADD) and Attention-Deficit Hyperactivity Disorder (ADHD). I suppose this is the logical chapter to deal with these new understandings, but I certainly hesitate to refer to them as "disorders." They are "disorders" that have helped motivate many of our greatest artists, leaders and thinkers to change the world.

What is the difference between the two? Obviously the clue is in the *H*, which stands for *hyperactivity*. Those with simple ADD are less likely to experience that symptom; otherwise, these are both behavior patterns that are caused by an imbalance in certain chemicals that regulate the efficiency with which the brain controls behavior. They both involve two neurological problems: perceptual difficulties and short attention span.

Your ADHD grandchild will show a tendency to be inattentive to external guidance. She will be naturally impulsive and restless. The behavior isn't always "hyper," however. It can be quite the opposite. Teenagers become disorganized. They struggle to plan simple daily tasks. Inattentiveness and restlessness are no longer the main problems, but only secondary ones.

The younger child in particular will struggle to tune in to classroom activities or a task at home. Teachers and parents may perceive that she is restless, careless, lazy or clumsy.

We have to work much harder to fill the emotional tank of our ADD and ADHD grandchildren. They are restless and distracted; therefore we have to make certain that our love really comes across to them. We also have to guard against becoming impatient and focusing on the frustration that their behavior causes us. We find ourselves saying things like, "You never stay on task," or "You are the most disorganized person I've ever known. Don't you take pride in your work?" Even when the ADHD has been diagnosed, and even when we've been educated about the symptoms, we forget ourselves and react to the typical behavior patterns. And that makes the ADHD child feel worse about herself. Her life can easily become a difficult cycle that feeds into a struggle with self-esteem.

Need I remind you that our love is unconditional? We don't love our children simply when they think and act as we do. We love them, *period*. We also recognize that now is the time when they need our love more than ever.

I want to emphasize that careful and thorough counseling should be sought if you believe your grandchild suffers from symptoms of ADD or ADHD. Having made that clear diagnosis, a doctor may recommend a medication such as Methylphenidate (known as Ritalin, Metadate or Methylin). Adderall, a mixture of dextroamphetamine and laevoamphetamine salts, is also becoming prevalent among prescriptions. However, be aware of up-to-date research. New medications and diagnoses are currently in development. If you or your grandchild's parents can apply the appropriate prescription, you'll find a marked improvement in attention span and the other struggles of this behavioral style.

A good doctor will also show you how there are many changes that can make life easier with ADD or ADHD. We need to rearrange the lifestyle and environment to be more helpful to these tendencies.

Most of all, however, we need to be positive. Talk about the heroes of ADD and ADHD. Your grandchild would be in good company with Einstein, Mozart, DaVinci, Disney, Churchill, Ford, Hawking, Edison and so many other luminaries throughout history.

Disorder? It's more a matter of "thinking differently." We can choose to look upon it as something truly special, a pathway that God has provided for true pioneers. Even as you treat your grandchild, and even as the frustrations are mitigated, the advantages remain.

## YOUR GRANDCHILD AND BULLIES

Playground bullies have been around forever. But in these angry and confused times, their number has increased drastically. We now have a considerable problem with predatory behavior in our schools and neighborhoods. Is this a disorder like the rest? Not quite; it is something else entirely, but it is a problem that we should stop to address.

It may be a problem you're unlikely to hear about, because pride keeps children from admitting to being bullied. Little boys in particular worry that their fathers will think they aren't "tough" enough, and therefore they suffer in silence.

Why do some children bully others? Generally speaking, they come from homes in which punishment-based discipline produces them. This is yet another negative byproduct of parenting that begins with behavior rather than love.

A grandson could be the target of physical bullying if he is small in size or shy socially. A granddaughter could be the target of psychological bullying if she is perceived as not fitting in. Boys and girls have different ways of establishing dominance over those they see as weaker in some way. Be aware that you may have to ask the right questions, including asking teachers and other leaders, to discover whether bullying is a problem in your grandchild's life.

A child will often believe that the bully can't be stopped, or that adult intervention will exacerbate the problem, or even that he somehow deserves to be bullied—this can happen if his self-concept is poorly developed. Some children don't believe that a parent or grandparent would understand, since they're not there when it happens, nor do they know the bully or bullies.

In the case of a younger child, work with the parents to involve teachers or others who may be in a position to help. In the case of a teenager, be sure to involve the child herself in the solution. Let her express her opinion on the best way to handle things. Remember, your long-range goal is for her to have the confidence and maturity to handle her own problems.

Your most important strategy, of course, is to keep the lines of communication open. Encourage your grandchild to talk about his day when he comes home. Ask leading questions such as, "Did you get along with everyone today? Any problems?"

If a physical attack occurs, the issue becomes far more serious. Depending upon the severity of the situation, you will certainly want to notify the police and the school itself.

## SPECIAL NEEDS, SPECIAL LOVE

We could discuss other disorders, disabilities and special needs if we only had the space. Whatever the challenge may be, parents and grandparents will receive the love and the grace they need to handle it. In the end, of course, the need itself is not particularly special; it is the child who is truly special.

Parents and grandparents need to do a much better job of networking with their community in all the needs of parenting. In most larger towns and cities, you'll find groups of parents who are also facing the challenges that you face with your grandchild.

Above all, keep your grandchild's emotional tank full at all times. Make sure that you offer plenty of eye contact, physical touch and focused time, and that the child's parents do the same. It's remarkable to discover the extent to which a well-loved child will overcome any obstacle; but one who feels unloved is equal to few tasks.

As a grandparent, you have the benefit of the long-term perspective that your children and your grandchildren aren't capable of seeing. Your years of life and wisdom have shown you just how much we are shaped by our challenges. In the New Testament we find these comforting words from James:

Consider it pure joy, my brothers, whenever you face trials of many kinds, because you know that the testing of your faith develops perseverance. Perseverance must finish its work so that you may be mature and complete, not lacking anything. If any of you lacks wisdom, he should ask God, who gives generously to all without finding fault, and it will be given to him (Jas. 1:2-5).

When your adult children come to you in tears, bringing the special needs of their children, you can be a voice of calm, comfort and godly perseverance. You know that the Lord will use all these circumstances, even the worst of them, for the good of the grandchild. A bout with depression, provided we overcome it, can lead the sufferer to a wonderful sensitivity to the emotions of others someday. The challenges of ADHD can mean unique creative contributions to the world. The child who defeats his fear will emerge with courage great enough for all the threats that lie ahead in life.

In the grand economy of life, Christians believe that nothing happens without meaning. Our God is a loving God, and He does not bring these problems upon us. It is an unhealthy world that does so. What God does provide is His presence, His power and His wisdom. And it could be that much of the time He will provide those very things through a loving grandparent who can be present in the flesh, who can provide power for healing through financial and other resources and who can offer wisdom from the journey of life.

He wants to use you in the life of a precious young person. Isn't that a wonderful, energizing thought?

# 10

# Grandparenting and Faith

Bob leans forward eagerly from the center of the church's second pew. He wears a smile as wide as his face can produce. If they would let him sit on the front pew, where the ushers sit, he'd be there. He is one proud grandfather.

Bob's grandson, Jeremy, is making his debut as a musical performer. Oh, by the way, there are 11 other 5-year-old vocalists sharing the spotlight with this remarkable, singular little boy. Bob thinks the "supporting cast" is nice enough, but he only has eyes for Jeremy—second row, third from the left—who is the very image of Bob's daughter.

The crisp burgundy-and-white choir robe seems to swallow little Jeremy. His head appears to be so small that it may not even be visible from the back pew. And that's why Bob arrived an hour-and-a-half early to stake out a good seat. He has brought his video camera to document the entire gala event.

The children enthusiastically half-sing, half-shout the words, "His banner over me is love!" They point to the sky for *His*, use their hands to trace out great imaginary banners around them, and add the traditional cradled-hands sign for *love. Just look at those smiles*, Bob thinks. *Listen to their pure joy at standing together to sing to their parents, their congregation and their Lord.*

Bob sighs deeply, closes his eyes and shares a quick conversation with the One in whose honor this facility was built. "Lord," he says, "thank You! That's all I can say, so let me say it again: Thank You! Here and now, sitting on this pew and listening to these little fellows sing their anthems—who would have thought this would be the culmination of my life?"

For a fleeting second, Bob's thoughts roll across a mindscape of personal moments: his graduation from high school, his wedding day, the birth of little Jeremy's mother—and then he remembers that he was praying. "Yes, dear Lord, I realize now that it can't get any better than this. There was a time when I thought a million dollars would make me the happiest I could be. Or maybe it would be my dream job that would fulfill my heart's desire. I even believed that if I could only be *young* again somehow—and stay that way—it would be the most wonderful thing I could imagine."

Bob looks up briefly to see that the choir is now singing "Zacchaeus Was a Wee Little Man." He continues, "Now I look before me and see something a million dollars could never buy. I see that I've already performed my dream job: raising my wonderful daughter. And I see something better than being a child again; I see the image of myself through the image of my daughter through this beautiful five-year-old boy. Through him, I can live beyond the day I die. Through him I can touch the future. Thank You, Lord, for giving me what my heart wanted all along. Amen."

Bob opens his eyes and is a little embarrassed—but only a little—to see that his daughter is peering at him from the next seat. Her eyebrows are lifted in curiosity. Bob gives her a warm smile and squeezes her hand, then turns back to the presentation. The children are recounting in song how Jesus looked up at the wee little man and said, "You come down from that tree!"

Bob realizes that these children will store the tales of Jesus in their sharp young memories forever, because they have memorized them in the days of their youth. What a wonderful thing it is to take a child to church, just as his young spirit is being formed!

That thought gives Bob a surge of hope for the future. And with a full heart, he thanks God one more time.

# FAITH OF OUR (GRAND)FATHERS

What is the place of faith in your grandchild's home? That's a concern for many grandparents I know. They look at this problem-plagued world and they see the challenges that face children growing up in it. Many grandparents, having stood strong in their faith through the decades, know the importance of spiritual belief.

The problem is that we haven't done the best job passing the torch to the next generation. Those who are over 50, studies show us, are far more likely to regularly attend church than are younger people. We want our children to know the God who has blessed us over the years. Then, when we become grandparents, the need suddenly becomes more urgent. Surely our grandchildren will be trained in an environment of faith.

We know one thing for certain. If we raised our children to be active, devout believers, they are far more likely to return to faith with their own children. Those who are products of spiritually less passionate homes will be harder for the church to reach.

There is another pattern that has held true through the decades. A certain percentage of young adults will drop out of church and seem less committed to their faith for a season of their lives. Their parents will worry about them and question themselves on where they went wrong as parents. Then, when their children marry and begin their own families, they will show a revived interest in what the church has to offer. In other words, they will want their children to have the same faith experiences they themselves had.

The church alone, of course, is unlikely to do a full job of spiritual training. Children truly believe and incorporate what they learn from their parents in a loving environment. In other words, young parents who drop off their children at Sunday school, then return to pick them up—never mentioning God or faith at the dinner table during the week—won't receive the result they expect. Faith is caught before it is ever taught.

On the other hand, these young parents often find themselves drawn into the world of the local church because of their children. Pastors know that as the kids go, so go the parents. Minister to the little ones and sooner or later they'll have the opportunity to minister to Mom and Dad.

As we talk about the faith of your grandchildren, therefore, we must begin with the generation in the middle. If you've raised your adult children to believe, congratulations! You've taken the most important step. If your children aren't currently active in church, patience is a good place to begin. If they are younger parents, or if they're expecting their first child, there is a good chance they'll discover a renewed interest in faith on their own. Nagging them, of course, can have the opposite effect.

What are some other obstacles? Perhaps your adult child has had a bad experience with a church. People seem to hold grudges *ad infinitum* against churches. Perhaps the church where you raised your children is no longer relevant to a younger age group. Let's think about the topic of churches themselves.

## THE CHURCH SEARCH

If you're interested in your children and grandchildren discovering or rediscovering church, you could get the ball rolling by doing a little research. What churches can be found near the neighborhood where this family lives? Look for a thriving congregation that your child could reach by car in 15 minutes or less.

If you call some of these churches, look for fellowships that have lots of children. These are obviously the ones that are doing the best job of ministering to young families. If you go for a visit, look around to see who else attends. If it's largely a gray-haired congregation, you might be more comfortable there than your young adult child would. As you may know, we have quite a generational split in today's church. Younger fellowships have largely turned to more contemporary worship forms, including music played by bands and a more informal setting. Remember, you're shopping for a church for someone from the next generation, not from yours.

If your grandchildren are very small, visit the nursery and childcare facilities. Are they clean? Are there safe monitoring systems for children and the adults who work with them? Many churches today require special bracelets or other forms of child identification to ensure that it is really the parent who retrieves the child. Some are also doing background checks on anyone who volunteers to work in the nursery. At a church, of all places, we want to have peace of mind that our grandchildren will be safe and secure.

If your grandchildren are teenagers, ask questions about the youth ministry. I've had plenty to say over the years about the importance of good youth leadership and activities at church. Working with teenagers is the most difficult job in the ministry, and that accounts for the rapid turnover of personnel in that field. Find out if there is an experienced youth pastor and a full slate of activities to keep your grandchildren interested, going and growing.

In recent years, I've also begun to urge young adults to ask for important information about the church they're considering. For one thing, you should request a statement of theological beliefs. What does this church accept about the person of Jesus, about the Bible and about the other essentials of the faith? Also, it has become more important to know how an individual church is led. Is the pastor accountable to a board? To a denomination? We simply can't make quick assumptions.

We need to know all the essential information about a place of worship before we can entrust it with our beloved family. Imagine what would happen if you succeeded in getting your children and grandchildren actively involved before having a negative experience? This could have a poor impact on the faith of your grandchildren.

A wise grandparent, then, will do his or her homework. Find the best church that has a convenient location, the right spiritual foundation, sufficient activities for the relevant age groups and worship that will win their hearts. Then you might invite your adult children to bring the family and visit with you. Tell them you've been hearing wonderful things about this church, and you'd like to see what they think about it. Finally, ask God to move in the hearts of that young family. All the salesmanship and persuasion in the world will be unsuccessful if the Spirit of God doesn't draw people to Himself. Commit your loved ones to the Lord, invite them and let God do the rest.

## "GRANDMA'S CHURCH"

When grandchildren come to visit us, we love to take them to church, don't we? We've been telling all our friends how marvelous our grand-kids are. We've showed them wallet pictures and told funny stories. Now we want to bring them on Sunday and really show them off. But can this be a point of tension with the children's parents?

As we've agreed, there are situations where our children don't attend church regularly themselves. It is far more common than ever before for our children to marry outside their faith. That makes it possible for grandparents to unwittingly create tension in the marriage by taking grandchildren to church. Given this situation, some grandparents wonder if they should avoid the entire issue.

My advice is to think of the welfare of the grandchildren. We need to work with the parents to help the child be exposed to the right influences; it's simply a matter of being sensitive, courteous and cautious in approaching the situation. Always ask the parent before taking the child anywhere, including church. Parents will appreciate your coming to them first, and most of the time they'll give permission.

If you live near your grandchildren, the opportunity is even better. I've seen many grandparents regularly bring their grandchildren to church, with the children becoming active and enthusiastic participants. Quite often the children's parents are later drawn into the fellowship and even make professions of faith to become Christians themselves. As long as you are working with their parents' approval, this is a wonderful plan and a powerful opportunity to impact the faith of your grandchildren.

Again, your chances of being successful are better if you attend a church that does an excellent job ministering to young families. If you plan to bring your grandchildren with you, call in advance. Let them know you're coming, and that it's very important to you that your grandchild have the most wonderful and enjoyable experience possible. If your adult child plans to attend with you, make doubly sure that members of that church who are the same age will be especially friendly, perhaps inviting your adult child to a Bible study class or some other event.

## Train Up a Child

Even when you can't take the child to church, never underestimate the powerful effect your personal influence can have on a child. Throughout this book we have established that grandparents represent crucial sources of stability, wisdom and love. Grandmother and Grandfather are sacred to the heart of a child. The place they live is a kind of "holy ground." Therefore, all that you do and all that you say will be engraved in the memories of the children.

Faith, as we know, is more than going to church. It is the grace and living testimony of all that we do. So consider the model of Christian faith that you present for your grandchild. Does he ever see you reading your Bible? Do you offer a simple prayer before meals or—better yet—do you ever suggest a prayer of thanks when God does something good in the life of a child?

Many grandparents buy colorful children's Bibles and storybooks to read to the younger child when the child comes to visit. As he grows to be a teenager, of course, you'll have to find other ways to make an impression. Consider this important passage from the Old Testament:

> Love the LORD your God with all your heart and with all your soul and with all your strength. These commandments that I give you today are to be upon your hearts. Impress them on your children. Talk about them when you sit at home and when you walk along the road, when you lie down and when you get up. Tie them as symbols on your hands and bind them on your foreheads. Write them on the doorframes of your houses and on your gates (Deut. 6:5-9).

If you love God this way—with your whole heart, soul and strength—then your faith will speak for itself. It will be quite obvious in the way that you live, which will be so attractive that your grandchild will want to live with the same joy and grace. Jesus, of course, added a corollary: "Love your neighbor as yourself" (Matt. 22:39). Show your grandchild how to care for others as Christ would care for them.

Though your faith will speak for itself, this passage from Deuteronomy instructs us to speak for our faith as well. It says to engrave God's Word on our hearts, so that we can teach it to our children as we sit together at home, as we take walks or drive to the grocery store, as we say goodnight at bedtime and as we rise for another day. His Word, these voices conclude, should be written all over our lives and our residences.

The "politically correct" line today, of course, is to avoid "indoctrinating" our children (and that, of course, is a doctrine in itself). If we don't teach about our faith, we are teaching the absence of it. Let's imagine an extended family where (tragically) the parents have no spiritual beliefs, but the grandparents are devout. The child is at a disadvantage in religious training, but the grandparents have a powerful opportunity even so. Those children will see the difference in the lives of the grandparents. He or she will see that Grandma and Granddad have a joyful, friendly fellowship of church friends that fill their life. He will see that the little things—a sandwich for lunch, bedtime at the end of the day—all have significance because God is involved with them.

I hope and pray that your adult children are followers of Christ (and that you are, as well). Even if they're not, God can and will use loving, obedient grandparents to make a difference with the grandchildren.

## MOMENTS WITH GOD

Here is a question to ponder: If you could teach your children one lesson about God and one only, what would it be?

For me, the answer is easy. I want my children and my grandchildren to know that *God is love.* In the same way, my greatest goal as a parent was to fill my children with love. I knew that if they felt well loved and accepted, they would go on to live full and successful lives. If you can only teach your children that God is love, they will always be attracted to Him, and they will always seek Him. People today don't always realize this obvious, biblical truth from the apostle John: "And so we know and rely on the love God has for us. God is love. Whoever lives in love lives in God, and God in him" (1 John 4:16). Some people hear that God is a father, but this model isn't the best one for them because they have not had good fathers. Some people are taught that God is wrathful and judgmental; therefore, all they have is fear.

But the one noun in the Bible that can complete the sentence "God is _____" is *love.* It is the most powerful description of Him that we can make, and it is the one most likely to attract your grandchildren or anyone else to Him. Someday, when you've moved on to a far better place, and your grandchildren are adults, what will their memories be like? We want them to think of their grandparents' home as a place of warmth, music, laughter and, particularly, *love*. We want them to think, "Our grandparents loved God and it showed in the way they loved everyone else."

That's why you need to make the God-link. What do I mean by this? When there is a wonderful moment, bring the Lord into the subject. All should be to the glory of God anyway, so make that a practice. When you've had a wonderful day with your grandchild, sit together at bedtime and say, "Aren't you grateful that God gave us this beautiful day? Aren't you happy that He loves us so much that He would have us enjoy ourselves like this?"

I remember a fishing trip in North Carolina with my two sons. We were having so much fun that we kept fishing even after the sun set. As we sat out by the water, we saw the moon and the stars come out. What a clear night it was! These days it's so much harder to see the stars unless you go way out into the country. But that night, there were all the constellations in their ancient glory. We could see the Milky Way itself.

As we sat quietly and took it all in, I think we all had a chill run down our spines. I began to talk about the marvel of God's creation. I remembered how the Bible said it: "The heavens declare the glory of God; the skies proclaim the work of his hands" (Ps. 19:1).

It was Dave, my older son, who said, "It makes me feel so *small*."

"Me too," I said. "When we think of the greatness of the universe, we do seem tiny. Yet our God cares about the very hairs on our heads. Did you know that? He knows every little detail about us, even more than we know about ourselves. And sure, a constellation is tremendous in size compared to you and me. But which do you think He loves more—you or a collection of stars?"

The boys sat quietly and thought about my point. We could feel God's presence.

I said, "I'm thankful that One so powerful is also so good."

Now Dale spoke up: "*Why* is He good, Dad?"

"I don't know," I replied. "My mind isn't big enough to take all that in. But I know one thing for certain: I know He loves me, because I can feel that love. And I can see these two amazing gifts He gave me, the two of *you*. I think He enjoys being with us right this moment, just as we enjoy being with each other, under this starry sky."

I can tell you that none of us has ever forgotten that moment. I didn't plan it, design it or orchestrate it—it came about because we wanted to catch fish. Don't you think God will present that kind of special opportunity to you as you spend time with your grandchildren? Ask Him to give you and show you the teachable moments when you can make a memory that will last a lifetime. Those are the very moments when living faith is born.

## OTHER OPPORTUNITIES

It's fascinating to me how our grandchildren watch us. They are so interested to discover what the mommies and daddies of their mommies and daddies could possibly be like! And in most cases, there is no one in their world more important to them, no one who stands taller in their estimation, next to their parents themselves.

As they watch us, and as we have moments to spark their young faith, here are some of the opportunities that will present themselves to us.

### Spinning a Good Yarn

What comes more naturally to a grandparent than storytelling? Grandchildren love to hear about our experiences from a different era. Perhaps you can regale them with accounts of life as it was amazingly lived without a personal computer or a game console. Like Jesus, you can find parables in the common items and events of life. There are also opportunities in the ongoing events in your personal story and in the life of a child. For example, imagine that you're taking your grandchild to the grocery store with you. On the way, you pass a certain fast-food chain that isn't open on Sunday. You can ask your grandchild if he knows why that might be so. It happens, of course, that the founder of the chain is a Christian and wants to make a statement about his faith by closing his business on Sunday to honor the Lord on the Sabbath. You can ask what your grandchild thinks about that. Why would someone give up all the money he could make on one of only seven days of the week?

Many grandparents, of course, have medical challenges. We tend to worry over our health and our medication, and we love to verbalize our longing for the days when our bodies were so much younger and fitter. But what an impression you could make on your grandchild if he saw that you didn't worry at all about this. You could say, "Oh, I've got a perfect body just waiting for me! You see, the Bible teaches that in the next life, we will live in bodies that don't need glasses or braces or hearing aids or corrective shoes. Isn't that exciting? I can't wait!"

You don't need to be overly pedantic or to make every single experience into a teaching event, making it all begin to look contrived. Instead, simply wait for those special moments when God gives you a special memory or current experience to work with.

## Problems and Solutions

Nothing makes a greater impression on children (or on anyone, for that matter) than the way we apply faith to life. I've already made the point that your very attitude about your health can present an inspiring view of powerful faith. What about other problems that come up in your life or the life of your grandchild? Each one of these is a test case for the validity of what we believe. What if, on that same trip to the grocery store, some car cuts in front of you to steal your parking place, and your grandchild says that his dad gets really upset when that happens? You can point out that as a Christian, you believe in forgiving people when they hurt you in some way. You can point out that we don't know much about that other person who may have a lot on his mind, or who may not have seen Granddaddy's car. (Do this, of course, without criticizing the child's father.)

The more you offer such a refreshing point of view, the more your grandchild will bring you his problems. You then have the opportunity to teach and to guide him. Talk to him about the wise and loving way to approach problems with his grades or among his friends. Help him see how delighted God is when we solve problems His way.

Examples of humble service also make wonderful impressions. Let your grandchild see how you serve others. Take him for a visit to the hospital, where you encourage and pray for a friend who has had surgery. Look for ways that he can help you help someone else—grandchildren love feeling helpful. In each case, point out that we love others because God first loved us.

## Optimism and Hope

This is a dark and cynical world. When your older grandchildren hear the voices of gloom and doom telling them that this is the final generation, that the world is ruined, and that life is pointless, you have the opportunity to show them that wherever God is, there is always hope. There is nothing that He cannot do, and everyone who turns to Him will be blessed.

Teach your grandchildren this verse: "'For I know the plans I have for you,' declares the LORD, 'plans to prosper you and not to harm you, plans to give you hope and a future'" (Jer. 29:11). There is nothing you can do for your grandchild that is more important than showing him that love, peace and hope for the future all lie in God. So many depressed and suffering children today have been damaged by this negative, anti-child, anti-Christian culture. But we have the truth on our side. That truth is that God is not dead, nor has He stepped away from this planet. He loves us as He always has, and our children need to turn back to Him.

"So do not fear, for I am with you; do not be dismayed, for I am your God. I will strengthen you and help you; I will uphold you with my righteous right hand" (Isa. 41:10).

Throughout the Bible, whenever God sends someone on a mission (Abraham, Moses, the prophets, Paul) He promises them two things: His presence and His power. One day the Lord will walk with your grandchildren into that future, hand in hand. And He will give them all the strength they need to face whatever lies around that next corner.

Until then, it is your charge to prepare them, to help them meet that wonderful Lord. A little child may be afraid of the dark, but he will say, "I will go if you'll go with me and help me, Grandma." Someday, when we are gone, we want our children to say, "I believe that God is someone like my grandparents—someone loving and wise, someone patient and powerful. I don't mind walking into the darkness, because I know what it's like to walk with someone who will hold my hand."

# The Legacy of a Grandparent

Maxine softly closed the front door and turned around to look at her empty living room. Her house was suddenly so quiet. Bill, Julie and Christine were on their way back home.

Maxine walks to the sofa and rearranges the embroidered cushions. She lifts an empty glass from its coaster on the end table and straightens the throw rug with the turned corner. Now that Christine is getting to be such a young lady—12 years old!—there are no longer scattered toys to put away. It's a little sad, because Christine was so adorable as a little one. But it's nice to see her sit beside her parents with a big smile and join in the conversation, just like her parents. They're doing such a good job with her.

She walks down the hall to the homey little room she uses as a study. Seating herself at the desk, she picks up the little framed picture of Christine, removes the photograph from the frame, and slides in the brand-new one that was taken at school. She stops to compare the two; only a year's difference, yet how quickly she has grown and changed. Here at the age of 11, Christine is just a little girl; here at 12, in this new picture, she is quite the young lady.

With a sigh, Maxine wonders how quickly another year will fly by and another picture will show startling changes. Even as Christine becomes more lovely, the grandmother knows that she herself will show a few more wrinkles. With each year there will be a little less energy and a few more health challenges. As someone said, aging isn't for sissies—

but it certainly beats the alternative. Maxine chuckles to herself as she remembers that line.

She has raised this subject with Christine's parents, Bill and Julie. They wave it away awkwardly as young people will do, saying, "Hush your mouth, Mom, you'll live forever! You're as young as you feel." What else can they say?

It doesn't matter; Maxine is perfectly at ease with the subject. All of us grow older, and the trick of it is to do so gracefully. Maxine's father didn't do that. He was terrified of old age, and he made few preparations for retirement or even for his passing. As a result, his estate was a mess on the day when he went to be with the Lord.

That had taught a hard lesson to his daughter. She was going to be prepared for the future with no nonsense about this illusion of living forever. Her house would be in order and everyone would know what would be left to them, and there would be special provisions for Christine, her only granddaughter. God willing, Maxine would see her off to college. What an exciting day that would be!

Bill and Julie could afford tuition and board at the state university, but Maxine had put away a few dollars to be certain the girl could go to school wherever she really wanted. "You take care of the grades," Maxine had said, "and your grandmother will come up with the money."

She had also thought carefully about her estate. She'd had a living will, of course, and she had thought that was all she needed. It was fairly simple, the lawyers had helped her draw it up and sign it, and that had been the end of that.

Or so she had thought. Six months ago she had read a disturbing article in a magazine about the so-called "death tax." It told horror stories of inheritances being lost almost totally to taxes. Could this be possible?

Maxine found a specialist, an estate planner, and looked into the fate of her financial legacy. It was hard to believe that, as things stood, the government would get 73 percent of her modest wealth! She was not about to let that happen. Her estate planner assembled the right financial consultants and lawyers, and she had a new will drawn up. This one would guarantee that the government would get the least possible helping of all that she left behind.

Not that she was against taxes in general—she had always paid them with a smile on April 15, as a good citizen should. Nor was it about leaving her child and grandchild "rich." Maxine wasn't in that league by a long shot! She did have enough to help her granddaughter have the educational opportunities that she really needed. She saw such a legacy as an investment in the future—and the dividends would be paid in the quality of a young life.

That's what Maxine really cared about these days. *Some of my friends dwell on the past,* she thought. *Me, I think about the future. I want to know that when I'm gone, the fruit of my life can still be doing some good.*

And how better to do that than through a beautiful, intelligent and gifted grandchild?

## How to Live Forever

I'm not the first to say it: Time keeps passing, and none of us are getting any younger. Those of us who are wise, realistic and loving give a good bit of thought to the future. We want to be certain that we provide for the needs of those we love, knowing that we won't always be here to care for them.

There is a high degree of contentment in knowing that there is indeed a way that we can live on, even after we pass on. We can invest ourselves now in the people and things that we care about. We can establish trusts and financial legacies that can be designated however we want. We can provide for our children and our grandchildren, as well as churches and charities that mean something to us. I counsel every adult to think carefully about how his or her estate can be invested in the future toward our most precious desires.

I had precisely the experience that Maxine did. For years I lived under the naïve assumption that I had made the necessary arrangements for my last will and testament. I'm eternally grateful to have discovered just how wrong I was about such a vitally important matter. As I write these words, I've just recently signed the final papers that will guarantee that my estate is dispersed in such a way that those I care about most will receive the most benefit.

It's a sad fact that fewer of us are leaving as much as we desire to our loved ones. Tax laws have had something to do with this, along with skyrocketing health-care costs that can totally consume a life's savings in almost no time. If you would like to do the greatest service to your adult children, convince them to start planning their finances now. Help them see that if they expend the bulk of it now on luxuries, their children could be deprived of the education they need.

Those educational costs have also soared. That's why grandparents need to step forward and do all that they can to establish educational endowments for their grandchildren. The wonderful thing is that we can designate our funds, giving us the peace of mind that they will be spent on the university or on whatever our personal values dictate.

Are you absolutely certain that your will is up to date, and that your estate is protected to the maximum degree from unnecessary government taxation? If you have any degree of doubt about this matter, don't procrastinate a single day. Find the most excellent estate advisors that you can and educate yourself on how best to design your living will.

Finances, of course, are only one of the legacies that we can leave behind. Let's look at some other ways that our lives and work can be blessings to those we love.

## ENDURING CHARACTER

Occasionally, we see the child of a departed friend. We're struck by the genetic legacy—the family resemblance that endures through the child. *He has his mother's eyes,* we'll think. Or, *She has a way with words just like her father.*

This is one of the many reasons that children are a blessing. They take the baton and continue to run the race for us, and they carry with them our resemblances, traits, traditions and memories. However, we also leave something that is more important than eye color or musical talent. The qualities of character and integrity will surely constitute our greatest legacy.

Grandparents so often take the lead in teaching and exemplifying integrity. Children watch us carefully to see what type of people we are. When they observe honesty and good citizenship in the way we handle life, it makes a great impression. Simple things go a long way. For example, imagine that you take your grandchild with you to visit a friend in the hospital. The little girl sees how gentle and attentive you are to someone who is ill. She sees that it's important to you to take time to minister to someone in need.

Then, in traffic on the way home, there is an accident somewhere ahead of you on the road. Your grandchild can hear the horns honking, and she can see the anguished faces of the impatient drivers in other cars. You can take that opportunity to teach a lesson about patience and grace—with or without words.

If you are married, how about the example of how you treat your spouse? When married grandparents are loving and affectionate together, it makes a profound impression that grandchildren never forget. This would be particularly true if the child's own parents don't get along well. It would be easy to gather a negative impression of marriage, as so many young people today have done. But grandparents can offer an alternative view—a living example of how wonderful it can be when partners for life truly give themselves to each other in love.

I should mention that it's possible to teach negative lessons too. How do various forms of bigotry, for example, get passed from generation to generation? We see what our parents and grandparents believe, and we tend to take on their values. "If it's good enough for Grandpa, it's good enough for me." Therefore, we need to remember at all times that our grandchildren are watching. We can teach important lessons in character, honesty and integrity.

## ENDURING LOVE

There is no more important legacy to leave with your grandchild than the legacy of love. It begins, quite obviously, with the love that you give the grandchild herself. If you help the parents in keeping her emotional tank full, you will have taken the greatest step in leaving behind you one human being who is capable of providing healthy love to others.

It's interesting to observe what items are identified by the Bible as being eternal: God, people, God's Word, His law and His love. Paul says that faith, hope and love are things that remain—but the greatest of all is love (see 1 Cor. 13:13).

Why do I mention this? In my opinion it is love that is the fuel of the human spirit. It is the greatest power in the universe, and all that God does is done through His magnificent love. It follows that giving love should be at the center of all that we do as well. That's why I've spoken of an emotional tank throughout this book. It needs to be filled and refilled with love and acceptance, because it tends to run dry quite often. In an increasingly dark and unloving world, the love you give your grandchild can make all the difference.

If you can show her what love is, she will have the one thing that casts out all darkness, heals grief and gives meaning when life doesn't seem to make sense. Truly your love is a gift that will keep on giving.

Yes, it's true that the child's parents must be the primary teachers of love, and of everything else. But parents have such a difficult task today. They will struggle with the challenge of raising and training a child. At times, they may not give the child all the love that she needs. You, as the grandparent, can stand in the gap. You can provide a supplement of wonderful love and support for both your adult child and your grandchild. Sometimes, when they are upset with each other, your love can be the power that helps to heal the wound.

## ONE GRANDPARENT'S LEGACY

When I think about grandparents, my mind always goes to Ken, a friend of mine.

Ken and his wife, Debbie, were wonderful parents who raised an outstanding, gifted and intelligent daughter. Unfortunately, the daughter made one bad decision that changed her life and the lives of many others. She fell in love with the wrong man.

After a short time, this husband left her with two children—just vanished with no thought toward caring for his wife or his two little ones. The daughter, an accomplished nurse, was left to support them herself. But she could not control her schedule at the hospital. There was no way, for example, that she could get her two children to school, because of her nursing schedule.

For years, Ken rose at 5:30 in the morning and drove the two kids to school. At the end of the school day, he would bring them home again and care for them if his daughter could not be there. He and Debbie took care of every need their grandchildren had, essentially filling in for a deadbeat dad who abandoned his responsibility. In so many cases today, the abandonment of a parent leads to a tragedy: children who feel unloved and thus cannot live happily in the world. They have no model of what a loving father is like, feeling deserted and resentful as they do.

In the case of Ken and Debbie, however, these grandparents stood in the gap. They gave of themselves sacrificially because they loved their daughter and their grandchildren. Today's result is two beautiful, happy and successful children who will make a positive impact in this world. The grandparents lit a candle rather than curse the darkness.

I close with the story of Ken and Debbie because it teaches two very important lessons. One, obviously enough, is that grandparents can make the difference between tragedy and triumph. The other is that grandparents must care for themselves, too. Ken did not do that. In one of the earliest chapters, I wrote about assessing our own health and fitness for taking on the task of parenting. I want to mention it one more time for you because it is so important. My friend could have done all that he did *without* sacrificing his own health needs. All he needed to do was reserve a little bit of time for visits to the doctor and living a healthier lifestyle. If he had done those things, he would still be here to enjoy his grandchildren, his marriage and even my friendship.

What about you? Can you make a more positive impact in the lives of your grandchildren? Will you care for your own health?

More than ever I believe that grandparents are a very special gift from God to a hurting world. They are like ministering angels who come from the last generation to this one to take the hand of little ones and help them walk through the darkness. The best people I know in this life are grandparents. As you devote your own life to this sacred calling, my prayers go with you.

# Postscript

By Cami Ross

Can you imagine growing up with an acclaimed family counselor for a grandfather? That idea might make you squirm a little bit. You might expect that such a relative would always be squinting his eyes at you, stroking his chin and examining everything you said.

Thank goodness it wasn't like that for me! My grandfather, Dr. Ross Campbell, has helped thousands of parents and children all over the world. Millions of copies of his books are on bookshelves. But for me, he'll always simply be Grandpa Campbell—the best grandpa anywhere. As for my grandmother, though she has passed away, I carry her with me in my heart wherever I go.

What I have loved best about them is the way they were always there for me. In some of my earliest memories, there they are—perfect playmates, dependable sources of love and affection.

Here's another good thing: the way their love grew and changed and adjusted itself to every age and stage of my life. When I was very little, of course, it was all about big hugs and playing together. My grandfather made me laugh like no one else in the world could. He had a different "funny face" for every feeling: sad, angry, silly, and so on. When you're a little "drama queen" as I could be at times, that was just the right thing.

As I struggled to grow up, his funny faces helped me learn not to take myself quite so seriously. In a really shrewd way, I think he was teaching me to stop and have a good laugh at myself. It would have been harder for my parents to do something like that, but it's one of those great things about grandparents.

My grandfather loved telling me stories and acting them out. His stories often had little lessons carefully hidden in them, and I learned all kinds of things without meaning to!

He also had what he called his "tortures." In his vocabulary, that was just another word for tickling! He had a whole arsenal of them. You haven't lived until you have experienced the Song Torture or the Indian Torture (which turned a tomahawk motion into a tickle attack). I could always tell when he was coming for a good tickle, and I would begin to squeal before he ever got to me!

Then, of course, I began to grow a little older. Teenagers don't go in so much for tickling—and yet again, my grandparents knew just what I needed. They were a safe haven for stormy times.

As a college student now, I can look back and appreciate the love my parents gave me and the patience they had with me. We all go a little bit crazy when we move through those years, and I guess we make our parents crazy, too. They were loving and wise, but I had a few turbulent moments when even they couldn't help. I suppose that's why God made grandparents.

In particular, I remember how I was struggling to figure out high school and how I fit into it. There were a few times when everything simply bubbled up inside me until I needed to escape. I just couldn't be in my home, even my bedroom—the television, the computer, the phone, the friends, the parents. I needed to get away from everything that was tangled up with my life and my frustrations. I was thinking, *Stop the world—I want to get off!*

There was no way to stop the world, so instead I had to find a special place where I could escape the stress I was feeling. I asked Mom and Dad if I could stay with my grandparents for the night. They're so great; they understood, even though I knew they wanted to reach out, pull me in and try one more time to fix my problems themselves. I know that someday I'll feel just as they did, and I hope I can be as wise and as gentle.

When I arrived at my grandparents' home, there was a hot bubble bath waiting for me. My grandparents knew me well enough to have just the right thing. The guest room was ready, with the sheets pulled down and the curtains drawn. Everything was quiet, calm, peaceful. My grandparents knew how to be just near enough for security, just far enough to give me space. There were moments when I just needed them to hold me quietly, and somehow they always knew when those moments had come. My home, my friends and my problems seemed a million miles away.

What I remember most of all is how much love I felt in their home. Like so many teenagers, I usually felt unlovely, confused and awkward. But I had no doubt that my grandparents loved me unconditionally. Their hearts were as open to me as their front door. There was nothing I could do to lose the love they had for me.

Outside our own homes, who but a grandparent knows us so well and loves us so deeply? Who else can be both perfect friend and wise mentor? My grandparents' home was a safe haven for me. In that rugged season of my life, I slept deeply, rested emotionally and found the measure of healing I needed. When the morning came, I felt stronger and more whole. I knew that I could go home, face school, return to my friends and confront any problems that troubled me. I really don't know how I could ever have made it through without the loving grandparents with which God blessed me. They were my rock and my fortress.

I want to mention one final thing. My grandmother fought cancer with grace and spiritual strength. In doing so, she taught me a lesson I will never forget. I saw her calm assurance that the Lord was caring for her, and I knew that if I can someday possess a faith that is anywhere near as powerful as hers, I will have succeeded in life. In the end, the cancer prevailed, but I cannot say that it won the battle with my grandmother. As she moved on to the gracious reward for her life, she taught all of us how to face that final inevitability like a victor.

As I struggled to come up with the words for this tribute, I realized I had already written one—all the way back in seventh grade. In closing, maybe the best thing I can do is to show you how a little girl felt about her grandmother at the age of 12:

## GRANDMA CAMPBELL THE GREAT

Bump! Bump! Bump! As Mom, Dad and I go up my grandmother's long driveway, filled with rocks and sticks, we look at the environment. There is a cardinal sitting high on top of the big oak trees that tower above us. Sometimes we are lucky enough to see deer, wild turkeys or even a red fox cross the road. When we approach the beautiful, complex house, I think to myself how picturesque it is, just sitting in the middle of nature. It seems to be saying, "Come on in, Cami, and have a great time!"

Cooper the Dog comes up to greet me when I get out of the car. I go into the house and a rush of excitement surges through me as I anxiously run to see my grandma. She is always in the kitchen, cooking us up something delicious! Not only is she a marvelous cook, but she is also a great teacher who has taught me some of the most important things in my life. She has taught me to be favorable, caring, and to have strength.

My grandma has taught me the importance of doing favors for other family members. She cooks all the holiday meals for my family. Also, she plans many parties for people with birthdays, anniversaries and many other occasions. Grandma lets me help her out with the parties by letting me wrap presents and make party decorations. This makes me feel good because I am having fun, yet helping someone out at the same time. Grandma has done many things to show how much she cares.

Grandma has taught me how to care for others. When people get sick, she buys presents for them and they really appreciate it. She also makes the weak or hurt feel better inside by comforting them with her words. She runs errands and does favors for people, too. These things really make me admire, respect and look up to her, and I want to do the same for others.

Likewise, my grandma has shown me how strong she is. In March 2001, she was diagnosed with breast cancer for the second time. At first, her cancer wasn't so bad, but then it spread to her lungs. Our whole family was very depressed at this news, but Grandma just comforted us and said everything would be all right. Grandma had to go through chemotherapy. The thing that amazed me most, though, was that she never complained. She prayed about it. Similarly, her husband travels a lot, but she doesn't complain about that either. She is just happy that he gets to go and see different places. Strong in the heart, Grandma never gives up.

If you read this, you will see how wonderful my grandma is and how much she means to me. Her house is just like her. She tells me to come on over and hug her. She provides shelter for the heart. She is in the middle of the woods, the only one of her kind. There are too many good things about her to name. I love Patricia Campbell, my grandma!

Shelter for the heart. That's what I love best about grandparents. At this early stage, it's hard for me to imagine it, but I just might be a grandparent too someday! If and when that happens, I will have courage, because I've been trained by the best.

For now, however, I get to enjoy loving my grandparents. I enjoy sending and receiving text messages with Grandpa Campbell; I send "heart messages" to Grandma Campbell, because I know she is somewhere else, enjoying that ultimate shelter for the heart, where someday we'll be together again. I don't know what heaven is like, but in my imagination it's a lot like the safe haven my grandparents always provided me. Maybe that's the best lesson of all.

# Five Ways to Get the Most from this Book

**Down the Block.** Do other grandparents live on your street? Invite them for a weekly discussion of this book's content over coffee. Each week you can discuss a new chapter. You'll enjoy building relationships with fellow grandparents—and when the study is complete, your friends will find they've become a close-knit support group for advice and encouragement. If you're parenting your grandchildren, you might want to focus on others who are doing the same.

**Over the Weekend.** Have a "Getaway for Grandparents" weekend re-treat. Hit the book's key points for group sessions, small-group interaction and a closing time of prayer and commitment. A concentrated weekend focus on the material will give it extra impact, and you'll come home refreshed and rejuvenated, ready to apply your new understanding. Again, the special challenges of parenting a grandchild may provide a terrific focus for a weekend group.

**In the Classroom.** Study a chapter per week with your adult Sunday morning class. *How to Really Love Your Grandchild* can become a practical and rewarding group curriculum. Class members will enjoy comparing notes from their grandparenting experiences each week—and reporting the week's progress in applying what they learn.

**With Your Spouse.** For a very personal one-on-one study experience, study each chapter with your spouse. Plan, and protect, an uninterrupted hour once or twice per week for reviewing the chapters and applying them to the special challenges of loving your grandchildren. You'll grow together as a couple even as you grow into wiser grandparents.

**Over the Internet.** Start a "Great Grandparenting" bulletin board (such as a Google group or Yahoo group) and invite your friends to log on and share insights as they work through the book. Long after your study is finished, grandparents will want to continue sharing their experiences and assistance in your Web group.

# Study Guide

Use this chapter-by-chapter guide to enhance your growth as a grandparent. The questions are designed in such a way that you can use them in your personal study, in discussion with your spouse or in a more formal group learning experience with fellow grandparents. Note the three kinds of questions provided:

1. *Start.* The first question for each chapter is a general (and gentle) way to begin thinking about the chapter's topic. It will help you or your group recall personal experiences that relate to what we'll be discussing. In a group session, this question is a good icebreaker—that is, it makes it easy for participants to jump right into the discussion.

2. *Study.* These questions—five or more of them—move you through the main points of each chapter. Their goal is not only to help you clarify the key ideas but to also begin thinking about how they will help you as a grandparent.

3. *Strengthen.* Each chapter's final question will motivate you to consider how to put these truths to work during the next few days. These may be the most important questions of all; so if you study this book in a group setting, be certain you leave enough time to discuss the *strengthen* question.

Chapter One:
# New Grandparents for a New World

## START

What are some important aspects that make your grandchildren's daily world different from your own childhood?

## STUDY

1.  Describe some of the ways that modern culture and the media ignore the character formation needs of children.

2.  What are some ways that the community at large assisted in child-rearing in the past? Why has this behavior ceased?

3.  List some ways the community can again influence a child's behavior in a positive way. How can you as a grandparent make a difference?

4.  As our culture continues to cater to the baby boomers, how has this contributed to a "child-unfriendly" environment?

5.  What are the basic needs of your grandchild? How can you meet those needs?

## STRENGTHEN

Describe your current three greatest fears about grandparenting. Based on the concepts mentioned in Chapter 1, how can you be more encouraged and effective as a grandparent this week?

Chapter Two:

# Helping Mom and Dad

## START

Is your adult child comfortable asking you for help, in your opinion? Why or why not? In what ways have you provided some form of assistance in the past?

## STUDY

1. When the rules of parents and grandparents appear to be in conflict, what are some of the issues that arise? How does this conflict affect the grandchild?

2. How can parents and grandparents create an environment of unquestioned love and harmony when disagreements between them arise?

3. List some reasons why it is important not to go against the wishes of your adult child in the parenting arena.

4. What steps can you take to ensure that you and your adult child do not compete for the affection of your grandchild? Why is this important?

5. How can you determine what parenting issues or rules are important to your adult child?

## STRENGTHEN

Brainstorm two or three ways that you can show love, support and encouragement to your grandchild's parents during the next two weeks. Make a plan to do it!

Chapter Three:
# Grandparenting from a Distance

## START

How far apart must grandparents live from their grandchildren to be considered "distance grandparents," in your opinion? Why?

## STUDY

1.  What are the advantages of setting up a regular time to phone your grandchild rather than simply include the child in a regular family phone call?

2.  Why is it important to supplement phone calls or emails with a more traditional written letter to your grandchild?

3.  What special ideas can you think of for a care package to send to your grandchild?

4.  What are the advantages of physical togetherness over long-distance communication?

5.  During an extended visit, what are some enjoyable activities you could pursue with your grandchild?

## STRENGTHEN

As either a long-distance or up-close grandparent, what are your plans for staying in touch with your grandchild during the next few months?

Chapter Four:
# Parenting Your Own Grandchildren

## START

What do you think is the greatest challenge of parenting one's grandchild? Why?

## STUDY

1. What are some explanations for the rapid increase of parenting being done by grandparents?

2. How would you go about evaluating your physical and emotional readiness for taking on such a task?

3. Summarize what are, in your view, the most important physical considerations for a grandparent's health.

4. What are the most important emotional demands of grandparenting?

5. How can you as a grandparent enlist help from your community in carrying out the task of parenting?

## STRENGTHEN

In which of the areas of fitness (body, heart, soul) do you feel strongest in caring for others? In which do you feel weakest? Explain your answer.

Chapter Five:

# The Love Your Grandchild Must Have

## START

How would you describe your personal need for receiving love on an everyday basis? Who provides it for you?

## STUDY

1. Why do you think love is the most basic need of any child?

2. Why is it that a grandparent can make such a unique contribution in providing love to a child?

3. What is different about the ways that children and adults receive love?

4. How is a loving environment created in a household?

5. What important reminders help us to be patient with children so that we won't withhold love?

6. What are the three ways of filling the emotional tank?

7. What should we remember about giving gifts to our grandchildren?

## STRENGTHEN

What are your best ways of giving love? Which can you improve on with your grandchild?

Chapter Six:
# The Anger Your Grandchild Expresses

## START

How was anger handled in your original home—through confrontation, avoidance or discussion? Explain.

## STUDY

1. Why is anger management training so difficult for a parent?

2. What are the primary vehicles for expressing anger? Which do children use most often?

3. What are unconscious influences within us? What is "stealth anger"?

4. How can punishment become a self-perpetuating cycle—a "trap"?

5. Several proactive steps are suggested for preparing to handle anger. Which do you find most helpful? Why?

6. What is the worst form of anger? Why?

7. What is the "anger ladder"? Explain.

## STRENGTHEN

Think carefully over where you can identify anger in your recent family experiences. What steps can you take to improve your approach?

Chapter Seven:
# The Discipline Your Grandchild Needs

## START

How did your disciplinary approaches as a parent differ from those with which you were raised, if at all? In comparison, how do you think your adult children approach discipline?

## STUDY

1.  What is the difference between discipline and punishment? Define each term.

2.  Discipline for any child should be based on what reality? Why?

3.  What are some physical issues that may lead to misbehavior?

4.  Name the five keys for correction. Which are negative and which are positive?

5.  When is spanking effective? What are its dangers?

6.  What is behavior modification? What is its basic flaw, and when, if ever, could it be used?

## STRENGTHEN

What disciplinary issues would be helpful to discuss with your adult child?

Chapter Eight:
# The Protection Your Grandchild Craves

## START

How did you protect your child from the world's bad influences? How did that protection change in time?

## STUDY

1. Why is it that parents and grandparents should be "shrewd as snakes and as innocent as doves"?

2. What are some ways that grandparents can teach children to think maturely?

3. What are three components of integrity?

4. How can grandparents pass on their values to their grandchildren?

5. What is an "I-message"?

6. Name two powerful times for teaching a young person.

## STRENGTHEN

Write out a short summary of the values and ideas you would most like to pass on to your grandchild. Write these in the form of a letter to give to your grandchild at the appropriate time.

## Chapter Nine:
# The Special Needs of Your Grandchild

## START

What experiences have you had with children (yours or someone else's) with special needs? What important truths did you learn?

## STUDY

1. Are there more special needs than ever, or are the needs about the same? Explain your answer.

2. What are some of the special challenges of fear and anxiety?

3. What are the different ways that boys and girls deal with depression?

4. Name some of the most important warning signs of depression.

5. Describe the differences between the most common eating disorders.

6. What is distinctive about ADD and ADHD behavior in children?

## STRENGTHEN

What special gifts did God give you for dealing with the special nature of your grandchild?

Chapter Ten:

# Grandparenting and Faith

## START

What did you learn (or not learn) about spiritual faith from your own grandparents?

## STUDY

1. What is a common pattern of church attendance and non-attendance pertaining to young adults? What accounts for it?

2. What characteristics should you look for in a church suitable for your grandchildren?

3. What important steps should you keep in mind when thinking about taking your grandchildren to your own church?

4. In your opinion, what is the most important insight about spiritual training recorded in Deuteronomy 6:5-9?

5. What are some good times for teaching grandchildren about God?

## STRENGTHEN

What are your personal goals for creating a good spiritual model for your grandchildren?

Chapter Eleven:
# The Legacy of a Grandparent

## START

How do you view your personal legacy to this world in general? In other words, what do you hope to leave behind in influence, estate, and so on?

## STUDY

1. What is the most urgent truth to confront for anyone concerning his or her financial legacy? Why?

2. How can we leave a legacy of character? Give examples.

3. How can we leave a legacy of love? Explain.

4. What are two important truths to glean from the closing story about Ken and Debbie? Which is more relevant to your situation?

## STRENGTHEN

What do you consider to be the most crucial and practical truth you learned from this book? How do you plan to apply it as a grandparent? Write out a plan and make a commitment to be the best grandparent that you can be through the love and power of God.

# Other Resources by
# Ross Campbell

*How to Really Love Your Child*

*The Five Love Languages of Children*
(co-authored with Dr. Gary Chapman)

*Parenting Your Adult Child*

*How to Really Love Your Teenager*
(a Gold Medallion award winner)

*Kids in Danger*

*Getting a Clue in a Clueless World*

*How to Really Parent Your Child*

*How to Really Parent Your Teenager*

*Help Your Twenty-Something Get a Life . . . and Get It Now*

Remember Grandparents Day,
the first Sunday in September after Labor Day!

# More Great Resources from
# Regal Books

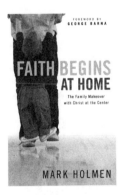
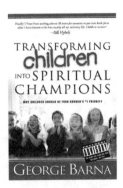